DIG YOUR WELL
BEFORE YOU'RE
THIRSTY

Other Books by Harvey Mackay

Swim With The Sharks Without Being Eaten Alive

Beware The Naked Man Who Offers You His Shirt

Sharkproof

DIG YOUR WELL
BEFORE YOU'RE
THIRSTY

The Only Networking Book You'll Ever Need

HARVEY MACKAY

Currency

Doubleday

New York London Toronto Sydney Auckland

For more on Currency and its resources, see information at the back of this book

A CURRENCY BOOK
PUBLISHED BY DOUBLEDAY
a division of Bantam Doubleday Dell Publishing Group, Inc.
1540 Broadway, New York, New York 10036

CURRENCY and DOUBLEDAY are trademarks of Doubleday, a division of
Bantam Doubleday Dell Publishing Group, Inc.

Rolodex is a registered trademark of the Rolodex Corporation
© 1990 Rolodex Corp.

Library of Congress Cataloging-in-Publication Data
Mackay, Harvey.
Dig your well before you're thirsty : the only networking book
you'll ever need / by Harvey Mackay.
p.   cm.
"A Currency book."
Includes index.
1. Business networks.   2. Social networks.   I. Title.
HD69.S8M25   1997
302—DC21   96-30025
CIP

ISBN 0-385-48543-3
Copyright © 1997 by Harvey Mackay
All Rights Reserved
Printed in the United States of America
May 1997
First Edition
1   3   5   7   9   10   8   6   4   2

DEDICATION

This, my fourth book, is dedicated to all the people who have stopped by to thank me after one of my talks . . . and to those who have stopped me in an airport to shake my hand or to share a great anecdote.

It is dedicated to all the kind folks who have written me letters, from 50 countries and in dozens of languages, with terrific advice and thousands of experiences in as many different settings.

It is dedicated to all the people who have phoned me, faxed me, and tickled their keyboards to send me E-mail, or visited my Web site, trading ideas and impressions in our fast-moving world.

It is dedicated to all those who have read my books, columns, and articles and found even one idea to stimulate and encourage them enough so that they have come back for more.

And it is dedicated to you new readers, whose first acquaintance with me has come from opening the covers of this book.

One and all, I am proud to say that you are now part of my network, and I am part of yours. And what we make of that network—however high our aspirations take us—is up to us and us alone. I can truly say that it is all of you who have helped me dig my well.

CONTENTS

Contents

ix

Contents

x

Step Seven: Don't Fall In!

Step Eight: Minding the Well!

ACKNOWLEDGMENTS

Not everyone—no, make that *probably no one else*—has a sister with great editorial skills, the patience of Job, the critical eye of a microsurgeon, and the disposition and kindness of a best friend. Without Margie Resnick Blickman, I would never have written any of my books.

Lynne Lancaster, a lightning bolt of a mind, a rare wit, who is a veritable magician. She is indispensable to me. Everyone who writes a book should have a Lynne Lancaster on their Rolodex.

Ron Beyma. Remember his name, folks. Why? Because one day he's going to write a major book. He's one of the brightest, most perceptive members of my "round table"—and a good friend to boot.

Greg Bailey, my executive assistant. This man has been through the trenches with me . . . and *for* me. I hope those all-nighters at his desk bring him the good fortune he deserves.

Mary Anne Bailey, who is infinitely patient and truly a great proof-reader.

Vickie Abrahamson is the most creative person I know—and that's saying a lot. If you start a sentence, she can finish it—with wit, humor, and style. She's got it all.

Jonathan Lazear, my agent and friend. This is our fourth book together. The two of us have covered a lot of ground, and we've had a great time doing it. He is the best.

Scott Mitchell, the President of Mackay Envelope Corporation, is a man I knew to have many positive qualities. I didn't know, however, that he can read with a sharp, critical and perceptive eye. He helped make this what I hope will be a very satisfying read.

Linda Ferraro, who has been with me for ten years. She's dedicated, good-hearted, responsible, and a real supporter, almost twenty-four hours a day. Mackay Envelope is better, and so am I, for Linda's presence.

Neil Naftalin, for his witty and pithy advice and counsel: "What goes on the cutting room floor . . ." One good man makes all the difference. I found one in Neil.

Judy Olausen. If you haven't heard her name or seen her photography, you will. She may be local to my town, but she has an international reputation—and deservedly so. If you want the best photo, I *may* be able to get you in to see her.

Denny Lyon, a man who has an uncanny sense for "where the fish are."

Richard Mallery, who could have written this book himself. He's a great idea man who is also a great critic.

Rick Frischman, publicist extraordinaire.

Paul Brown, a man who has the rare combination of asking the right questions and brilliant organizational skills.

Arlene Friedman, Lisa Brancaccio, Mike Iannazzi, Amy King, Jackie Everly, Paola Fernandez-Rana, and Laurel Cook, all of Doubleday, my new home.

Harriet Rubin, my editor at Currency, who said, "Harvey, you were born to write this book. Who on earth is better at networking?" Thank you so much for the basic idea.

And finally, to everyone at Mackay Envelope. You've taught me a lot, and you have my respect and admiration every day.

INTRODUCTION
by Jack Kemp

Within the first few minutes of meeting Harvey Mackay, I discovered he was already an expert on the Jack Kemp worldview. He'd done his homework, and I've never forgotten it. Nor ceased to be amazed.

Harvey Mackay was born to write this book.

Why do I say that? Because for a decade he's been giving great advice to millions of people through his bestselling books, his speeches, seminars, and nationally syndicated newspaper column. And he isn't just talking to the MBAs or the Harvard Law School wannabes. He speaks to all of us—his wisdom runs the gamut—from what he calls "life lessons," and now, to networking.

He's a natural. He speaks both from his head and his heart, with a genuine voice that's rare; plus his war chest of practical information, all applicable to almost anyone's life, at any stage of life, has helped millions of men and women get ahead and stay ahead.

Now Harvey's turned his attention to the facet of his life that is without a doubt the primary talent that has made him so terrifically popular, successful, and an inspirational networker.

The best kind of teacher is also a student, and Harvey has always been both. He's always been prepared to win, and this book can help get the reader ready for a life of making all the right moves.

No matter what you're shooting at, you'll need all the networking bows and arrows that this book has to offer. It's an indispensable joyride that can take you anywhere you want to go.

So sit back, get ready to be entertained, and take in the take-home advice your mother or your father never dreamed of giving you.

This is the book that shows you how to achieve a permanent network in a Post-it note world. Read it, pass it on to a friend, or perhaps, one or all of your kids!

DIG YOUR WELL
BEFORE YOU'RE
THIRSTY

HAPPY BIRTHDAY, ZIGGY!

A friend of mine, Ziggy, threw a party for himself on his sixtieth birthday and invited my wife, Carol Ann, and me to attend.

It was a mob scene. There must have been 300 people there, and I didn't know more than a handful of them. When we finally worked our way up to the host, Ziggy gave each of us a huge bear hug.

"You're too skinny," he told me. "All that running. I checked the paper, and I saw you ran in the Boston Marathon this year. You gotta eat more."

He speared a kielbasa from a passing waiter and stuck it in my mouth. "Good?"

"Good." I gulped. "How've you been?"

"Today, October 20, is my birthday. Three days—no, four days from now, October 24, is your birthday. That's a Tuesday, but, of course, you were born on a Monday. October 24, 1932, was a Monday."

"Now, how did you know that?"

"You ever hear of idiot savants? Can't dress themselves in the morning but can hear a piano concerto once and play the whole thing from memory? Some of us do it with dates. You name a date, I'll tell you the day of the week."

"You're no idiot savant."

"Nice of you to say that, Harvey. No, you're right. I looked it up. It's something I do. No one else does it, so I do it. Kind of a trademark."

We finally broke away to give Ziggy a chance to talk to his other guests, and Carol Ann and I melted back into the crowd. At some point, I turned to a fellow I know and commented on how much I enjoyed Ziggy and how well liked he is.

"Oh, he just has the knack" came the dismissive reply.

Party manners aside, I wanted to shake that guy and let him know in no uncertain terms "This is not a knack or a gift. It's not magic. It doesn't just happen."

I don't get birthday cards from Ziggy every year by accident. He doesn't know the day of the week I was born because he's an idiot savant. He didn't know about my running in this year's Boston Marathon because he loves to scan lists of 35,000-plus names set in six-point type.

These are the result of a lifetime of caring about people, of learning about them, listening to them, spending time, and paying attention. It's the result of a lifetime of networking—that is, a lifetime of asking what you can do for someone else.

Too often we think the networkers we most admire were "just born that way." It's a myth. The best networkers try the hardest and give it the most thought.

What struck me the most about Ziggy's party wasn't just the number of people, it was the *variety*. Young, old, various church affiliations, different ethnic backgrounds, bankers and social workers, musicians and engineers, old friends, mentors. They were all there. You don't gather a group like that by accident.

So, how do you do it? Building a network is really a lot like digging a well. First, there's a decision. "Guess what? I might be thirsty one day. I just might need a well to draw on. I think I'll work on that." Then there's the homework—getting prepared to dig. (I know I'm forever telling people they have to do their homework. Probably it has to do with my mother being a schoolteacher.)

Then you have to actually get started. That's a hump a lot of people never get over in other areas of their lives. But the good news is, as far as networking goes, you've already started. You have friends, family, coworkers, teammates, neighbors, fellow church or synagogue members, and on and on. Now you have to expand and excavate from where you've started digging.

Most well-intentioned laborers of any stripe start out with gusto, applying the shovel lavishly, sweating profusely. Then they stand back and survey their progress. That's usually about the time they realize they need to hone their skills.

> *Like any new behavior, the more you practice the skills of networking, the easier it gets.*

Once you've got the skills in place, you can really let fly and dig deeper. Not mindlessly and not by rote, however. You've got to dig thoughtfully, creatively, and with a little class. That's how the network gets bigger and the well gets deeper.

Then there's the maintenance. Nothing a man or woman ever built stayed in perfect shape without a lot of TLC. Ditto your network. Staying in touch with contacts is as important as getting them in the first place.

And don't forget about pitfalls. You didn't dig this hard just to have the well cave in on you. None of us is immune to mistakes.

Luckily, you have role models to follow and people like me who have already made all the mistakes we'll ever need to make. Learn from us.

And as you become more proficient at the process, your well will deepen. You'll notice that you are reaping extraordinary, life-changing rewards and that you can pass them on to those you care about.

You'll also notice you're having a good time. In fact, you'll realize you've found the well of life—other people.

This book is organized into ten sections that will give you a process to follow so that you never, ever need to be thirsty.

And it contains personal networking stories from some of the best

well-diggers around—people like Muhammad Ali, Lou Holtz, Stanley Marcus, and Pat O'Brien, just to name a few.

It's in your hands now. Dig in!

M A C K A Y ' S   M A X I M

Up the proverbial creek? If you've got a network, you've always got a paddle.

JUMP IN, THE WATER'S FINE!

Chapter 1

A NETWORK NEVER SLEEPS

Our foursome had finished the usual Saturday morning round of golf. We were in the clubhouse doing the postmortem when Jerry said, "Last night I got a call. It was two in the morning. I won't tell you who it was because one of you might know him. He was semihysterical. His accountant had called him that afternoon and told him he was broke; his company couldn't make the payroll, and if he didn't retrieve the checks he'd written, there was a good chance he'd go to jail. The guy needed $20,000. The strange thing is, I hadn't talked to him in over ten years. He said the only reason he called me was that I used to be a close friend and that I knew he was a trustworthy guy. Well, I offered to lend him a few thousand dollars, but I didn't give him what he needed even though I could have.

"It got me thinking though," Jerry added. "What if it had been me? How many people could I realistically count on to bust a gut to help me out if I'd called them at 2 A.M.?"

"How many, Jerry?"

"Two, maybe three."

We went around the table. The answers were about the same until they got to me.

"Fifty," I said.

"Come on, Harvey! That's B.S."

"No, it isn't," I said. "I've been ready to make the kind of call that

Jerry got for nearly forty years. I never had to make it. I made fifty others like it instead. I've made 2 A.M. calls to find the absolutely best doctor in town in a family medical crisis; I've made them to get a valued employee out of a blackmail situation and to stop a customer not only from dumping me but to keep him from badmouthing me so totally that my business would be ruined forever.

"I know I've been to the wall at least fifty times, and in each one of those fifty times, I was able to find the right person to get me the help I needed.

"Ever since I was dumb enough to buy a bankrupt envelope company when I was just a kid, I've been building a network of people who I could count on and who count on me in case one of those 2 A.M.ers came around. I know I wouldn't have survived if I hadn't, and I'm proud that a lot of other people who made those kind of calls to me wouldn't have made it either if I hadn't been part of their networks."

I feel sorry for the guy who called Jerry, because it didn't have to come down that way. But the guy didn't stay in touch. He didn't prepare. He not only didn't dig his well before he got thirsty, he waited until he was dying of thirst before he even started clawing the ground.

How many names do you think he called before he called Jerry—a guy he hadn't talked to in ten years? Five? Ten? Probably even more. And with each call the odds grew longer against connecting, because he was getting farther and farther away from his real network.

Remember the Broadway show and movie **Six Degrees of Separation**? *The title refers to the fact that there's a chain of no more than six people that links every person on this planet to every other person.*

What if I want to meet the president of GE and sell him some envelopes? Well, if I know somebody who knows somebody and so on, six deep, I can be standing there in Jack Welch's office pitching #10s before we play our next round. That's a helluva network, and we're all capable of building one just like it.

But try to reach over the five people between you and Welch directly? Can't be done. That's Jerry's nonpal's way. A non-network. A rope of sand. If you dig your well and actually have a network, you're never going to be out on that sixth dimension all by your lonesome where all you get is busy signals and wrong numbers.

"Jerry, I just want you to know that if I get a late-nighter from you some day, the twenty grand will be in your account within twenty-four hours. By the way, what have you got for collateral?"

"What have I got for collateral? I remember catching one of those 2 A.M.ers from you, Harvey. I've been there for you."

"You're right," I said. "And that's all the collateral you need."

Jerry and I have been around forever. If we can keep our network going year after year, it isn't too late for you.

The *New England Journal of Medicine* has published studies showing that people who stop smoking, even though they may have smoked for decades, can cut their risk of lung cancer nearly to the same levels as people who have never smoked.

Same reasoning with networking.

The *Mackay Journal of Networking* has no published studies but cheerfully predicts that no matter when you start, you can build a network of people who will pick up the phone, ready to help, if you ever have to make a call at 2 A.M.

MACKAY'S MAXIM

2 A.M. is a lousy time to try to make new friends.

Chapter 2

SIX CONCLUSIONS TO BEGIN

"Knock, knock."
"Who's there?"
"Not you anymore."
—Dilbert
by Scott Adams

A few months ago, *The New York Times* ran a series of front-page articles on the devastating effects of downsizing on American workers.

Buried deep in the first article of the series was this paragraph:

As an officer in charge of operations for the Standard Chartered Bank, Mr. Allen had to dispose of one of the three currency traders in the Toronto branch. The consensus choice happened to be a woman who was indisputably the top performer, but had the weakest political bonds. "I knew she was the best in the department," he said. "But she had not networked. And I had to inform her that she was terminated. She looked at me with tears in her eyes and said, "But Charlie, you know better." I will never forget what she said and how she looked that day.

Charles Allen, the man who fired that woman, is still haunted by the memory of it. ("It is a mark on my character. I feel a lesser person.") Allen is a fine, decent person, the kind of person who thinks about the consequences of his actions. He attends religious services every day. He has plenty of time for it; he lost his own job recently.

The articles ran for an entire week. They did not make pleasant reading. Since 1979, more than 43 million jobs have been lost in

America. Though a greater number than that have been added, many are at lower pay. Among those people who have been laid off and have found new jobs, two-thirds are earning less.

When I finished reading the articles, I came to these conclusions:

1. Talent alone will not save you in today's economy.
2. The traditional advice—more training and education—will not save you.
3. The government will not save you.
4. No matter how self-reliant, dedicated, loyal, competent, well educated, and well trained you are, you need more than you to save yourself.
5. You need a network. You need *your* network. Every day. A network will help you deal with some of life's minor annoyances as well as your most challenging problems. Your network can provide role models, advise you, comfort you, provide you with financial assistance, intellectual and social resources, entertainment, and a ride to work in the morning.

   Without it, you'll have a hard time finding a client, making a sale, seeking a job, hiring the right employee. To say nothing of the personal stuff, like locating a competent doctor, buying a house, or deciding on a nursery school for your kids.

> *If I had to name the single characteristic shared by all the truly successful people I've met over a lifetime, I'd say it is the ability to create and nurture a network of contacts.*

6. I would share what I had learned from a lifetime of networking.

MACKAY'S MAXIM

No matter how smart you are, no matter how talented, you can't do it alone.

Chapter 3

MAYBE NETWORKING REALLY *IS* ROCKET SCIENCE

As is true of many sales types, I am a refugee from science in all its myriad forms. Someone once explained to me how the laws of aerodynamics make it possible for a 870,000-pound airplane with 400 passengers to lift off and fly across the Atlantic. I still suspect the real reason is that God holds it in the palm of His hand.

I never imagined there was such a thing as a scientific study that proved the value of networking. I never imagined it because I couldn't imagine it.

However, there is one. In the *Harvard Business Review,* Robert Kelley and Judith Caplan wrote about a study they conducted of Bell Lab engineers to determine what attributes separated the 15 to 20 percent whom their peer group nominated as "stars" from the average performers. Daniel Goldman reported the results in his popular book *Emotional Intelligence:*

"One of the most important turned out to be a rapport with a network of key people. Things go more smoothly for the standouts because they put time into cultivating good relationships with people whose services might be needed in a crunch as part of an instant ad hoc team to solve a problem or handle a crisis."

Why does it matter that "stars" in science network well? After all, scientific superstars are supposed to be loner nerds in white coats who wear coaster-size eyeglasses.

It matters because superior technical networkers are the ones who:

- Know where the grants and the research money are available and know who controls the purse strings, so that they can get a fistful of the dough.
- Dial up the best people in their specialty to get an answer when they are stuck with a problem.
- Know how to get their patents and discoveries celebrated in the press to help them to become rich and famous.
- Are most likely to be confided in by their peers . . . and are therefore likeliest to become "hubs" in their disciplines.

Hey, so it takes me 300 pages to say the same thing.

Ain't science grand?

All together now, finish this sentence: "It isn't what you know, it's . . ."

MACKAY'S MAXIM

Networking may not be rocket science, but studies prove it works for rocket scientists.

Chapter 4

HARVEY'S TOP-TEN LIST
of the Most Important Things
a Network Can Do

t's not enough for me to convince you that you need a network. I want you to know *why*. Here are ten reasons:

1. **A network replaces the weakness of the individual with the strength of the group.**

Groups

The one that seems to be doing the best is the WASP Millionaires' Club.

Luckily for those of us not in that one, there are a gazillion others we can join. The idea is to benefit members who have the same race, religion, gender preference, ethnic background, business, trade and professional interests, economic interests, personal interests, you name it.

We all belong to some of these groups and probably should belong to more. They're the basic building blocks of any networking system.

If I had written this book five years ago, I would have suggested that people wanting to connect with a particular kind of group could find what they were looking for at only one place—the library.

But now you have the option: the library or the Internet.

You can be on-line instantly, communicating with people in whatever network you're interested in.

The benefits of this kind of networking have been hyped so much already, the only thing left is to sound a cautionary note.

Groups, be they the old-fashioned, meet-for-lunch-every-Wednesday types or the Internet variety, are ready-made for the group, not custom-made for you.

Like ready-made suits, they're not tailored to fit you individually but to fit some basic group prototype. If you're looking for a scholarly analysis of nineteenth-century Guatemalan postmarks or a rent-a-car discount, there's a ready-made group for you. If you're looking for the best urologist in town, or trying to find out whether your department is going to get axed in the next downsizing, you need your own personal custom-made group.

Not to say that you couldn't meet the girl/boy of your dreams at the next gathering of the International Society of Guatemalan Stamp Collectors; it's just that it wasn't designed to serve that purpose.

But while you probably could find out whatever information you needed if you worked at it long and hard enough, why reinvent the wheel? Join the group that has the experts you need.

2. Mirror, mirror on the wall.

A network is the magic mirror that can show you how the dress *really* looks on you before you wear it to the party.

Does the big report you've been sweating over the last two months make sense?

People who write or sell for a living, whether it's called "marketing planning" or "copywriting" or "just plain peddling," need to know if their stuff works. Who is going to tell you before you go out and make an ass of yourself?

Your network.

Get a network going to read your copy or listen to your presentation—in return for which, of course, you do the same for them.

Your network can identify what's unclear or confusing or simply wrong.

They'll catch the typos and grammatical errors you never dreamed you made. They'll tell you what's funny, what isn't, what's perceptive, what's offensive.

Don't think you need that kind of network?

Neither did Stephen Chao.

In 1992, Chao was a whiz kid at Rupert Murdoch's Fox Network. As Mortimer Feinberg and John J. Tarrant wrote in *Why Smart People Do Dumb Things,* he was a featured speaker at a management conference attended by Murdoch, the neo-conservative guru Irving Kristol, Defense Secretary Richard Cheney, National Endowment for the Arts Secretary Lynne Cheney, and others of that lofty ilk.

Chao decided to loosen up things a bit. He hired a male stripper to skinny down and shake his booty right next to Ms. Cheney.

Within hours, it was *Ciao Chao.*

Do you think Chao might have realized his little joke wasn't quite as funny as he thought it was if he'd held an undress rehearsal first?

Even if you're not planning to hire the Chippendales to do their thing at your next pitch, you still can use your network for batting practice.

Asking for a raise. Interviewing for a job. Presenting a report. Whatever it is: Your network can be your sounding board to learn what works and what doesn't. You'll avoid mistakes. You'll be helping others with the same needs as yours.

Now let's go to the flip side.

This time instead of being on stage, you're in the audience.

When you switch roles and become the critic, you're forced to analyze the performance. There's no better way to learn the tricks of the trade than by judging how others perform under conditions similar to yours.

After all, the other members of your network are making a living doing the same thing you're doing. Most people have their own little ways. Learning how *they* do it will help you improve how *you* do it.

3. Know thine enemy through thine network.

The *Godfather* movies reinvented the gangster genre by adding a new element to the usual rat-a-tat-tat stuff: Business Administration 101.

Michael Corleone doesn't say "I'm gonna get dem guys dat got my brudder."

Michael, our first movie business executive/gangster, says, straight out of Machiavelli, "Keep your friends close and your enemies closer."

Why should anyone do that?

Because, as everyone in business knows, you have to know what the competition is up to.

Who will tip you off if a key employee may be ready to jump ship to the competition?

Who can you count on to help you counteract someone circulating negative gossip about you or your company?

Who will tell you when others are making inquiries about you?

In government circles, this is called "intelligence gathering." We have great big agencies spending billions to spy on friend and enemy alike.

In baseball, it's called "stealing signs."

> *There is always a place in the dugout for anyone who can pick off the other team's signs.*

The first week I went into sales I spent the day with an old envelope dog following around a competitor's truck making envelope deliveries to customers.

"There's your prospect list," he told me.

Another tactic some businesses use is hiring their competitors' disgruntled employees or schmoozing with their suppliers—particularly if they also happen to be their competitors' suppliers—and getting the buzz on what's going on across town.

Is someone having trouble paying their bills?

Is there a key employee who's looking to make a move?

Are they having problems with any of their customers?

Are they active in the community? Do they participate in fund drives and volunteer work?

Do they value education? Do they encourage their employees to improve their skills?

How are they regarded in the industry? Do they attend trade shows? Are they involved in industry organizations?

You don't want to be the last to know.

There is no formal network for getting this kind of information. It can come from anywhere.

The one given, the one fact that never changes, is: People love to talk.

It's always smart to have some pipeline, however informal, into the enemy camp.

Suppliers. Bankers. Lawyers. Customers. Former customers. Employees. Former employees. Salespeople. Truck drivers. Spouses. Girlfriends. Car dealers. Bartenders at the cross-town factory's favorite watering hole.

PEOPLE LOVE TO TALK!

Keep your ears open. Information from your competitor's camp can come from anywhere, and it's pure, unalloyed gold.

This applies whether you're talking about corporations or individuals, business or personal relationships.

You hate them so much you never want to have anything to do with them?

No matter how you feel about the other guys, you could wind up doing business with them or at least gaining valuable information. Even the bitterest of enemies have been known to do it.

4. My network can help you expand your network.

A network isn't like a stamp collection—something that sits in an album that you take out and look at from time to time. It's not for show; it's for go.

One of the big mistakes you can make when you're starting your career is being afraid to use your network to ask for help.

Where to start?

There's Dad. There's Mom. But all their well-meaning career advice gets jumbled up with the other stuff about brushing your teeth and eating your broccoli. You need a fresh eye.

Whose?

Best bet: a family adviser, particularly a lawyer or a banker, a rich relative, one of your parents' bosses at work—anyone old, experienced in business, with a wide range of contacts and some personal or professional connection to your family.

Why? Because most so-called gurus and old fuds like me are downright flattered when someone asks their opinion—on anything.

We have fewer axes to grind. It no longer seems like every kid who walks through the door is trying to take your job away or waste your time.

Whether we've formally inscribed it or not, we have a network, and inevitably, it's going to evaporate along with us, and we know it. Still, we like being a player, and one way to do that is to pass along our time-honored war stories and offer a little godlike advice to whomever will listen.

That's the perfect setup for a young person who needs help and knows how to ask for it.

Make an appointment to see that "old friend of Dad's" at his office or home, if he's retired.

Of course, you're not going to see him to ask for a job. That would be too crude and obvious.

You want a little career advice.

Believe me, you'll get it.

At length.

And once you've gotten it, that old family retainer will have an investment in your future. Like contributors to a political campaign, people who donate help to you have a vested interest in seeing that you succeed.

Your failure would reflect on them, on the quality of their advice, and on their continued relevance.

Their network may be a little rusty, but it's probably going to be pretty powerful too.

A lot of young people have gone a long way by getting themselves adopted by an old tiger. The cub gets the benefit of the tiger's teachings. The tiger gets a disciple. Here are some examples:

Tiger	Cub
Saul	David
Julius Caesar	Mark Antony
Big Jim Collosimo	Al Capone
Bette Davis	Anne Baxter (*All About Eve*)
Henry Ford II	Lee Iacocca
Wally "Let the kid play today, I'm not feeling good" Pipp	Lou Gehrig
Woody Hayes	Lou Holtz

But tigers and tigresses beware. Cubs grow up and sprout claws. As you may have noted, not many of these cubs were content to remain in the shadows of their mentors.

5. A network can enrich your life anywhere in the world.

How many non-Americans are there in your network?

With phone rates, E-mail, and faxes measured in pennies these days, it's hardly any more costly to build a global network than a local one.

It's not tough to learn about customs and holidays abroad. Most places where you can find a greeting card will also sell you a global calendar so you know when to send it. I'll start you off with a couple of freebies: In Holland, St. Nicholas Day is December 6. In Hong Kong, Chinese New Year is always celebrated between January 21 and February 19.

One of the most powerful global networks is Guanxi, or overseas Chinese. There are 50 million people in this network, and they control huge wealth because of the importance that the extended family has to Chinese business.

In France, a huge percentage of the corporate bigwigs are graduates of the *Ecole Nationale d'Administration* or the *Polytechnique*.

In Israel and Switzerland, compulsory military service creates an important lifelong network—members have to serve in the reserve until they're fifty-five.

In Japan, graduation from Tokyo University's law school is the prized credential for career politicians or high-ranking bureaucrats.

In Poland, it's the Committee to Defend the Workers. Sounds like a classic Communist cell, but actually, the group has fought both the Communists and right-wingers.

And then there's that wonderful old-boy network in Russia—the Communists. They're just itching to stop reminiscing and start giving each other high-buck government jobs again.

Networking has always been crucial for immigrants. They use the strength of the group to gain an economic foothold in their new countries. If you live in an American city, you're bound to have noticed the number of self-help organizations that have sprung up among the growing Hmong, Laotian, Thai, Korean, and Vietnamese populations.

I've traveled with my wife, Carol Ann, to over seventy countries, and there's no emptier feeling than being in a foreign country and not knowing a soul.

There you are, alone, knowing you may never have the opportunity to be there again, with no one who can help you experience some of the real culture of the country, no one to invite you into their home so you can see how people actually live.

If you've got a network here, you can have a network anywhere. For openers, all it takes is one simple question to the people in your network: "Do you do much traveling?" All people love to talk about their trips, and they can literally open up the whole world for you.

Also, there's always someone *here* doing business *there.* How do you find them? Your banker will know. Additionally, you can get that information about almost any public company in their annual reports. Get those at the library or from your friendly stockbroker.

Or try the nearest university. You'll find students and faculty with contacts everywhere in the world.

If you're in school, the international student organization is a great place to start.

Why should they bother with you?

Because you'll make them part of your network. You'll hand-carry gifts, pictures, greetings, whatever to their friends and relatives, and you've been known to pop for dinner both here and abroad.

"*L'addition, s'il vous plait.*"

"*Die Rechnung, bitte.*"

"*La cuenta, por favor.*"

Maybe there are better ways to say it, but they always give me the check anyway.

6. A network can provide you with new experiences and knowledge.

I know a fellow who manufactured waffle irons. He sold his company for more money than he ever thought possible and retired at the age of fifty. By age fifty and three months, he was climbing the walls. He'd been a racing fan all his life, so he decided to go into the horse business.

The first horse he bought never made it to the track. The second and third were a little better. They earned modest sums before they too broke down.

The fourth horse was the charm. While he didn't actually make money on it, he entered it at several of the better tracks in the country, where it won a few races and lasted for several seasons.

Some people have pictures of their family on their walls.

He has pictures of himself with his horses.

Horse owners are a unique subculture. Many couldn't tell a hock from a stock. They compete with each other for goals that are essentially meaningless. Ninety percent lose money, and those who make money generally don't need it to begin with.

But still, you have only to look at the beaming faces in those winner's circle pictures to realize that the satisfaction of owning a racehorse has nothing to do with anything that makes economic sense.

It comes from being momentarily successful in a slightly glamorous, slightly naughty, enterprise far removed from the world of waffle irons.

"A good horse will take you to places you never dreamed of," Mr. Waffle Iron told me.

True enough.

Thus it is that even for those of us who stamp out waffle irons while fantasizing of rubbing elbows with the Willie Shoemakers of the world, there are networks to match our dreams.

7. Networking can help you help others.

Networking can be very rewarding for people who work the system on their own behalf. It can also be rewarding for people who work it on behalf of others.

Many alumni are active in recruiting promising students to their alma maters because they want young people to share the experience they had years earlier. Others enjoy giving career advice and counseling.

That's my bag; it's become my avocation. I've done this with over 1,000 young people in the course of a lifetime, and I get enormous satisfaction from hearing from them and about them later on as their careers progress. (But don't they ever need to buy envelopes?)

Charitable and civic organizations are desperate for volunteers, especially fund-raisers. The best fund-raisers are people willing to call their friends and associates and ask them for money—particularly if those friends and associates are wealthy and beholden to the callers in some way.

Not many people will do that kind of networking.

They don't enjoy making those phone calls, any more than anyone likes being on the receiving end and having dinner interrupted with a pitch for money.

If you are one of the rare types who are good at it, you can benefit a lot of people who need help.

You could also probably make a damn good living in sales.

There's a creative way to combine your efforts on behalf of individuals with your fund-raising duties.

When I'm asked for a favor, I'll often tell the caller, "I'll be happy to make a 'best efforts' attempt on your behalf—on one condition."

"Uh-oh. What's that?"

"If I deliver, then I want you to make a donation for $ _____ to
_____ charity." (I fill in the blanks based on the difficulty of the
task at hand and a kind of seat-of-the-pants rotation among the
United Way, the American Cancer Society, the American Heart Association, and a few others.)

Occasionally I'll have to haggle back and forth a bit, but no one has
ever said no yet. How can they, when they're asking for a favor for
themselves and I'm asking for help for their community? I can testify
that when I'm holding the hammer like that, there have been more
than a few audible quips on the other end of the line as they absorb
the price tag for the favor, but no one has ever turned me down.

Politicians describe giving personal help as "constituent work." It
involves acting as an ombudsman for people who don't have the clout
to get their concerns dealt with satisfactorily, particularly when they
involve a government bureaucracy. Veteran's benefits, social security
claims, admission to subsidized housing, recommendations to the service academies are all common areas of constituent service for members of Congress.

One phone call from the right pol is sometimes all it takes to get
matters taken care of. Doing these kinds of favors are the politicians'
stock-in-trade.

Know any pols? Most ordinary people don't, but guess what? Most
wealthy and powerful people do.

They know them, not because they are charming company, or because they need help battling the Medicare bureaucracy on behalf of
Grandma, but because pols do favors, not only for the less fortunate
but for the more fortunate.

Big favors.

And like other all-too-human types, the more favors you do for the
pols, the more likely the pols are to do favors for you.

You don't necessarily have to make a big campaign contribution.
Until they abolish door-to-door canvassing, lawn signs, and envelope
stuffing, there will be politicians who need your help.

Ask yourself this question: Do you think you might ever need
theirs?

If the answer is yes, then here's a network you might consider joining.

Political campaigns seek volunteers just as eagerly as charities do. But when you work for a pol, the ethics of how you do things are a little different.

Politics is a bare-knuckle business. No one takes the Boy Scout oath. Doing political volunteer work can be very demanding and very time-consuming and, unlike community organizations, which go on and on forever, when you work for a pol, you're a winner only if your candidate is.

The side benefits of volunteering come under the heading of Doing Well by Doing Good.

Volunteering for community organizations can put you in touch with the heavy hitters in town.

New kid on the block?

Poor but talented and ambitious?

The people who make up the boards of these outfits tend to be your community's corporate leadership.

Here's how you can get to meet them and show them your stuff: by making yourself—and your skills—known to them. By doing so, you're adding valuable contacts to your network.

As for pols, they're generally regarded as excellent personal references when you're applying for a school or looking for a job. If they win, there may even be a job in it for you.

8. Job security? Don't rely on the corporation. Rely on your network.

About the same time *The New York Times* was doing its series on downsizing, *Fortune* magazine was analyzing the same situation from a different perspective. The *Times* reported what was happening; *Fortune* told its readers how to survive it.

Stalin said, "A single death is a tragedy, a million deaths is a statistic." Because 40,000 layoffs also is a statistic, *Fortune* used individual case histories to give a human dimension to the problem. The magazine described the impact of the massive layoffs at AT&T on five of the laid-off employees and their families. Their prime example, a forty-three-year-old project manager named Paul Klemchalk, was featured on the cover. Klemchalk's sin? He was a "generalist." What the company needed was "specialists." He had been given sixty days to find a new job within the company or be let go. As the clock was ticking, Klemchalk described himself as "scared senseless." By the time the article was written, he'd already applied for fifty jobs and been turned down for all of them.

Fortune's take was that with companies depth-bombing entire departments, it no longer made sense to rely on your boss to save you. He or she may be just as vulnerable as you are.

The key?

Networking.

Cops, who are always at the mercy of the political winds, call it having a "rabbi," a superior in another department who watches out for them in return for loyalty and information. (I wonder if priests have "rabbis.")

To benefit, you'll want to establish ties across the entire organization. How? *Fortune* suggests you try to become part of a cross-functional team, a network, so you can get to know folks in other departments.

Well, that's fine as far as it goes, but what if there aren't any such teams in your company?

I'd say: Establish your own.

Your network can be formal or informal. That is, you can: (1) dream up a company-approved team project that operates through standard company procedures, that will put you into a close working relationship with people in other departments; (2) establish a "buddy system," a back-channel network of people who will watch out for possible slots in their area for which you may train or qualify in return for your doing the same for them; or (3) do both.

The AT&T announcement amounted to formal recognition that people who had networked, whether as members of company-authorized cross-departmental teams or simply as buddies, were the only ones who stood any chance of survival.

Not surprisingly, one survivor turned out to be the cover boy, Paul

Klemchalk. Two days before he was to be let go, he found a job within the company marketing phone equipment. Maybe he discovered a network he didn't know he had. Or maybe AT&T decided not to risk a follow-up article in *Fortune* describing their despondent ex-employee aimlessly pacing the floor of his "modest Cape Cod house" in New Jersey.

"Don't rely on the system," says *Fortune*. Amen, says Envelopeman.

9. A network can make you look good.

No salesperson who knew the names of his customers' kids ever went broke.

Knowing the spouse's name, unfortunately, is no guarantee.

You haven't seen your old buddy, Buddy, in a couple of years. You call him for lunch.

"How have you been, Buddy?"

"Great."

"How's Buddette?"

"Buddette ran off with her psychiatrist. They're living in Anchorage."

"Oh. Well, how's that terrific dog of yours, Squat?"

"Squat died. I have a new dog now, Grunt."

"Oh."

Not a pretty sight. I know. It's happened to me too. A name and a few scribbled notes on a 3 × 5 card do not constitute a network. You have to keep it fine-tuned or you're going to run into a lot of Buddy-type situations. Two years is too long between tune-ups.

You change your oil every 3,000 miles, don't you?

That's about once every three months.

Your car just gets you to work. Your network can determine whether or not you've got work to get to.

To keep your network up and running, freshen up each entry at least once every six months.

If you aren't actually sure whether Buddy and the last-known Mrs.

Buddy are still buddies, don't ask unless Buddy asks you about *your* spouse or mentions his. That's the best indicator that you're in a safe territory. Start off by talking about his kids. That gives him the chance to slip in any information he wants you to know.

10. A network expands your financial reach infinitely.

So far we've talked about networking among individuals.

Barter, sophisticated modern barter, is networking among corporations.

What makes it different from personal networking is that barter is networking stripped down to the bare essentials, cold-blooded tit-for-tat exchanges.

No idle chit-chat.

No Christmas cards.

No "Didn't we meet at the Coin Collectors' hoedown?"

Just bidness.

For five years I served on the board of Atwood Richards, the world's largest barter company.

Barter?

Everyone knows what barter is. That's cavemen sitting around the fire chewing the fat—literally—until one guy offers another guy a swap, like a bearhide for a spear and a couple of fish hooks. Right?

Wrong.

Barter, as practiced today by corporations, is light-years away from a simple Stone Age two-way exchange of goods. And it's probably the smartest, most cost-effective form of corporate networking there is.

Though corporate barter can consist of bilateral trade, in the real world such transactions are rare. It's unlikely to find two companies with simultaneous equal and opposite needs.

Let's say you run a United States–based chemical producer doing business in Africa. We'll call it the Chemco Company. You've agreed to take locally made sheets and pillowcases as well as a certain amount of production time at a weaving mill to satisfy an obligation. You have no use for 100,000 sheets and pillowcases, nor for the production time, nor do you have a clue as to how to market them.

Enter the barter company.

They happen to handle several hotel chains for clients interested in bartering.

Hotel company A winds up with Chemco's sheets and pillowcases. Hotel company B wants towels, and they want them with their monogram on them. Hotel company B winds up with the production time at the mill, where towels are made according to B's specs. Chemco winds up with room, food, and beverage trade credits for its sales force to use at hotels.

What are some of the other benefits of becoming part of the barter network?

Your existing channels of distribution are not disturbed. In fact, you may wind up with a whole new channel of distribution or a new marketplace.

You will quickly reduce costly warehousing and carrying charges.

Since you will be using your inactive products as payment for things you are now paying for, you will:

A. Increase your cash flow.

B. Reduce your cash outlay.

What can you use for barter?

- Excess inventory.
- Underutilized production time.
- Canceled projects leaving you with equipment you can't use.
- Countertrade obligations as a result of having to accept payment in goods rather than cash, typical when dealing with foreign companies.

What kind of companies are doing this?

How about Caterpillar, Amoco, Pfizer, JCPenney, Goodyear, USX, Exxon, Bell South, Monsanto? The list of companies engaged in bartering reads like a *Who's Who* of the Fortune 500.

When Peter Ueberroth headed the U.S. Olympic Committee in 1984, he put barter at the heart of his promotional efforts. He swapped the Olympic logo for airline transportation, for the use of 500 Buicks, for 250,000 feet of Fuji film plus processing, for Levi Strauss and Converse clothes and shoes. According to *Sales and Marketing Management,* he "even traded the logo for a swimming pool to be built by McDonald's."

Both financially and operationally, the '84 Olympics were the best in the history of the Games. I was in the audience when Ueberroth was introduced. It was the only time in the history of sports when 100,000 people gave a standing ovation to the guy who sold them the tickets.

Time is perhaps the easiest commodity to barter. Radio stations are notorious barterers, forever "trading out" commercial time for whatever it is their advertisers are peddling. Sometimes it's airline space. What a perfect swap! The radio station barters unsold time for an unsold airline seat. Neither party is out a dime. Both parties benefit.

Corporations understand that barter is a form of networking that can get you what you need for what you don't. And that's as close to something for nothing as you're ever going to find in this life.

Convinced? If not, keep reading. Knowing what a network is and is not will tell you what it can and can't do for you.

M A C K A Y ' S   M A X I M

If you're not convinced you need a network after reading this chapter, go back and read it again.

TIME TO PRIME THE WELL!

Chapter 5

PREPARE TO WIN

I've always felt that the real title to every book I've written is *Preparing to Win.*

That's what networking is about.

And selling, negotiating, and managing.

But that isn't what marketing is about.

Marketing is about packaging, not about the small print on the ingredients label.

Grabber titles are designed to sell books rather than provide accurate descriptions of their contents. Raise your hand if you think *Dig Your Well Before You're Thirsty* is about how to use a divining rod, and I'll see to it you get a full refund.

As a result, you are reading *Dig Your Well Before You're Thirsty* and not *Preparing to Win,* though the meaning of each title is identical.

I can change the words but not the music.

Recently, in Chicago, I appeared on a television round-table discussion sponsored by *Chief Executive* magazine. There were ten participants, every one of them CEOs of companies much larger and better known than my own.

Quite frankly, I had no business appearing with these big cigars, but thanks to some networking of my own, I was invited to participate.

Every step of the event was choreographed to minimize the

amount of time the participants would have to spend away from their important duties. The schedule was thirty minutes of hors d'oeuvres and cocktails; thirty minutes for a sit-down lunch; and thirty minutes for the shoot itself, a discussion of the technological revolution and how to turn it into a competitive advantage.

That was the magazine's agenda.

Mine was a little different. I wanted to use this little narrow window of opportunity to get acquainted with one or two people to whom I someday might be able to sell a couple of envelopes.

Obviously, once we sat down to lunch, we could manage to carry on a conversation, between mouthfuls, only with the person on our left and the person on our right with every word being heard by the entire table. When we got to the panel, it would be no better. We were programmed to perform for an audience of 40 million airline passengers who would be shown the tape of the show at 30,000 feet.

That left just the cocktail half-hour. The challenge here was to try to rise above the usual small talk.

I knew the magazine had bios on all ten participants, because they had me send in mine, so I called and asked them to fax me materials on the rest of the panel, which they graciously did.

Now I was prepared to prepare.

One of the CEOs was born in my mother's hometown of Virginia, Minnesota. Bingo. When we were introduced, the first thing I did was ask him whether he'd ever had a chocolate soda as good as the ones that Ben Milavitz's Drug Store, a Virginia legend, used to make.

Total amazement and instant credibility.

Another CEO had run the Marine Marathon in Washington the previous year. You don't put that in your bio unless you're damn proud of it. It just so happened that the week following the panel was the 100th running of the Boston Marathon. I said, "I bet I know where you're going to be next Monday at 9 A.M. Hopkinton, Massachusetts." So was I. For the same reason.

Result? Same as the Virginian.

"How on earth did you know that?"

I wasn't bashful. I told them about all the homework I had done.

I *always* make a special effort to inquire about people I'm going to meet and want to get to know better.

I could read in their eyes that the gesture was appreciated. Instead of a boring half-hour with strangers, they were able to connect with someone with whom they shared a deeply felt interest, a person they might want to meet again.

They benefited. I benefited. Even if I never sell either of them a single #10.

In the securities business, salespeople are required to perform "due diligence" on any new offering they sell. That involves acquiring an understanding of the company and its finances sufficient to be able to recommend the stock to an investor for whom it is suitable. That means you don't try to peddle hog-belly futures to widows and or-phans.

"Due diligence" is more than a legal concept. It is the means for making new friends, customers, and members of your network.

It is the way of life for anyone who wants to succeed in any activity.

Before you meet new people, before you make that call, do your homework. Find that common ground. Determine where their needs and interests lie. Make that connection.

By the way, I am now corresponding with one of the CEOs I met and have been invited to New York for lunch, a plant tour, and a helluva long run.

M A C K A Y ' S   M A X I M

Prepare to win. Then prepare to dazzle.

Chapter 6

NETWORKS, LIKE BASS, ARE WHERE YOU FIND THEM

I got my earliest lesson in networking when I was looking for my first real job.

First-place prize for dependency on networks goes to reporters. Their network of sources is their life support system.

My father, Jack Mackay, was the Associated Press bureau chief in St. Paul. He used to let me tag along occasionally when he made his rounds.

The places to go for hot gossip in those days were saloons and barbershops. At the age of eight, I wasn't up for the bar scene, but I was ready for Perlman's Barber Shop. For me, Perlman's attraction was an unrivaled comic book and sports page selection. For my father, it was a clientele of cigar-smoking, side-of-the-mouth-talking guys who always seemed to have the inside dope and guaranteed result of every upcoming local ball game, prize fight, murder trial, and political campaign.

There were five barber chairs in Perlman's. Seating arrangements were as rigid as for a state dinner. Seniority ruled. My father, who had been going to Perlman's since he was a cub reporter, was barbered by Perlman himself. He got chair one.

Every patron or hanger-on passed by my father going in or out of the place. He seemed to know each one of them, and they all had some gossip or a tip to lay on him. They say my father was a pretty sharp reporter. They also say he was the sharpest-looking reporter around. It figures. He got a barber shave and a shine every day, and at least one haircut and a manicure every week.

Not too high a price to pay for having the best network in town.

The day I graduated from college I began looking for a job. There were a lot fewer college graduates in those days, and I was cocky enough to assume I could start at the top and work my way up. After I had exhausted—unsuccessfully—all the possibilities my modest network provided, my dad said I should go see Charlie Ward.

Though my father seemed to know every politician and athlete in town, I had no idea he knew big-business types. Charlie Ward was not only the biggest of the big in St. Paul, but he was also the most colorful character around.

Ward was president of Brown & Bigelow, the world's largest manufacturer of calendars, playing cards, and anything else you could slap a logo on. In those days, it was called "remembrance advertising." Today it's called "collateral material" or "collateral advertising."

Four years before I graduated from college, Ward was in another institution of higher learning: "Greystone College." He was serving time for tax evasion. The Rise and Fall of Charlie Ward had been a huge story, and it was natural for my dad to interview him in prison.

Remember, my dad worked for the Associated Press, then and now a leading national news syndicate, so the story was carried in papers coast to coast.

The day after the article appeared, Ward got word to my dad he had to see him immediately.

Reporters tend to write about the seamier side of life, so they don't get many compliments from their subjects, particularly cons. My dad expected that Ward had found something to dislike in the story.

Still, Ward had been a good subject. Maybe there was a follow-up. My dad drove back to the pen, and Ward greeted him like he was the warden waving a full pardon. Ward loved the article. He was almost in tears, describing how Jack Mackay finally got the story right after all the nasty and inaccurate stories that had been written about him.

He asked my dad if he had any sons. (It wasn't in the cards in those days to inquire about a daughter. Women were expected to stay home and raise a family.) "One in college."

"When does he graduate?" Ward asked.

"When do *you* graduate?" my dad answered.

"In time to give him a job if he wants one. Have him come see me."

A promise from a convict? My dad didn't know if it was for real, but by the time I was out looking for a job, Ward was out too and back at the top of his game. So why not give it a try? (Note another difference between that era and our own: Accepting this kind of favor was not looked upon as a conflict of interest. Nowadays, if the higher-ups at AP had been aware that I was going to try to cash in my dad's chips with a news source, he would have been out of a job.)

I called Ward's office, managing to drop my father's name about three times in the course of the conversation with one of his secretaries, and got an appointment. The occasion justified my new Dapper Dan suit, the collar gapping about three inches off my neck. I had arrived by streetcar, standing all the way so I wouldn't ruin the crease in my pants.

"Mr. Ward will see you," said the oldest and sternest looking of the three secretaries who sat outside his office. I was ushered into a room which modestly could have held 250 for cocktails. Charlie Ward did most of the talking.

After some chit-chat, he uttered the magic phrase, "I'm going to put you to work in our 'goldmine' across the street . . . Quality Park Envelope Company."

After pounding the pavement for a month without raising any dust, here I was, standing in carpet up to my knees, being pitched not just to take a job, but a job in a "goldmine."

"Goldmine?" Well, it was kind of like a goldmine. It was cold, dark, and the implement I was using had a wooden handle like a miner's ax, only there was straw on the end of mine. There were also quite a few of Charlie's old classmates working there; he was a great believer in hiring ex-cons.

Still, it was a job, and forty-two years later I am still in the envelope business, still looking for that elusive goldmine.

Thanks, Charlie Ward, for both the job you gave me and the sales job you did on me.

Thanks, Dad, for my first lessons in networking. I've never forgotten them.

MACKAY'S MAXIM

Everyone you know, even if that person is wearing government-issued pinstripes, may qualify to be a part of your network.

Chapter 7

THE FOUR BEST PLACES TO GO PROSPECTING

Okay, you've decided to build one of the best networks the world has ever seen. You've started with your family, moved to your extended family—and their extended family—and then networked up, down, and sideways at work.

Now what? I would make tapping into these following four groups my next step, be it bowling, bridge, or helping kids sell cookies. The power of club membership is far reaching. It will propel your career— and change your life.

Alumni Clubs

Some universities have better alumni networks than others.

Graduates of the service academies are so tight with their classmates they're called "knuckleknockers," because of the large class rings they wear from the day they graduate until they run out of days.

The Ivy League has always had a well-deserved reputation as the mother church of the old-boys' network.

Both places are good, but I count three schools as the best of the lot: Wellesley, Notre Dame, and the University of Southern California.

Wellesley because the Wellesley network is the strongest female power structure in the country. Wellesley was preparing women to assume leadership positions in roles that had been traditionally reserved for men long before the rest of the world became aware that women were capable of performing these roles.

The headline in a recent article of *The New York Times* says it all: "How to Succeed? Go to Wellesley."

Wellesley women take up far more seats in executive suites and corporate boardrooms than their numbers suggest they should have . . . Evidence for the Wellesley edge abounds, starting with the number of companies that look to Wellesley for executive women. Seventy-five companies recruited there in 1994 . . . Of the 390 women who serve as directors of Fortune 500 companies at least 17 went to Wellesley—more than any other college.

Think "Hillary Clinton" and you have an idea of the kind of brilliant, tough-minded, loyal, successful graduate that school produces. There are thousands and thousands more. They include Secretary of State Madeleine Albright; Lois Juliber, president of Colgate North America; Ellen Marram, president of the Seagram Beverage Group; Shirley Young, a vice president of General Motors; Marion O. Sandler, co-chief executive of Golden West Financial; and Luella Gross Goldberg, who was acting president of the school for several months during 1993 and serves on the boards of several New York Stock Exchange–listed companies.

Notre Dame, because Notre Dame football is such a national treasure that everyone, it seems, Catholic or not, has two alma maters, their own and Notre Dame. Each alum is a lifetime talent scout for the school, and every Saturday during football season they all renew their commitment.

But the University of Southern California tops my list. There's the football thing, of course, à la Notre Dame, but there is also the well-worn description of the alumni network that fits it perfectly: the Southern Cal Mafia.

I don't know if they take a blood oath to help, hire, mentor, and generally take care of each other, but they act as if they did. From the day you graduate, the USC network is there for you. And, in turn, you, as a graduate, are expected to be there for other USC alumni.

USC has seventeen highly regarded professional schools. Their approach is unique. Students work more closely with mentors—living, breathing, out-in-the-real-world mentors—than they do at any other school I'm aware of. The USC faculty still teaches the fundamentals, but they also regard developing leadership as an essential part of their mission.

Every stereotype gets blown away. Mentoring relationships are not assigned on the basis of profession, gender, or race. When I served on the board of Warren Bennis' USC Leadership Institute, I was particularly impressed with a brilliant African American female dentist.

In my opinion, the USC alumni network is the tightest, most effective, and most closed to noninitiates of any alumni network in the country.

Industry Associations

Trade groups are happy hunting grounds for networking in all kinds of ways. If you're active in your trade club, you're in position to pick up major clues about what your competition is up to. Have a lot of the old gang from Company X dropped out recently? What's the buzz around the buffet table? Maybe Company X is on the verge of Chapter 11.

Many managers troll for executive talent at the local chapter of their industry associations. There's always a lot of gossip at these gatherings. If you're headhunting, it's a great place to find out which frogs may be ready to jump to a new lilypad.

I know of several new businesses that have been started by two or three people from different companies who met at industry association meetings.

Pat Fallon and Tom McElligott were working for different ad agencies when they began their business relationship. They called it "Lunch Hour, Ltd." That former seat-of-the-pants, after-hours business has become Fallon McElligott, twice named Agency of the Year by *Advertising Age* and one of the most successful and highly regarded advertising agencies in the country.

Social Clubs

Are golf clubs, social clubs, and athletic clubs important parts of a network? You bet they are. More deals probably are closed in these places than in all the offices in the country combined. (Well, maybe not quite as many, but how else to justify the time and expense to our spouses and our bosses?) Fellow club members are familiar faces, and there's a natural tendency to feel comfortable with people you see regularly.

The club is also invaluable as a place to entertain business associates or prospective customers. It's a lot less grueling and usually more convenient than having to entertain at home. (Maybe even less expensive. Have you ever figured what your true financial exposure is when you give your sixteen-year-old kid a few bucks and the family wagon and tell him not to come home until midnight?) It also has more panache than taking the One Who Must Be Impressed to a public restaurant. After all, it is Your Club.

Hobbies

Hobbies always have represented a great way to make contacts across a broad and diverse spectrum, because buffs often are scattered all over the map and can be found at all income, age, and social levels. Hobbyists tend to rate each other on their knowledge and hobby-related skills, so hobby networking remains pretty much a meritocracy, a nicely democratic way of evaluating your fellow human beings.

I'll use stamps as a metaphor for the networking potential of hobbies. Stamps go on envelopes. So when you're in the envelope business, there's a certain natural tug toward stamp collecting.

Stamp collectors may be somewhat less diverse than other hobby groups. They are usually males under the age of fourteen or over the age of forty-five.

Why the thirty-plus year gap?

Because at puberty, a young man frequently loses interest in stamps and becomes interested in ladies. By the time he reaches forty-five, the ladies often cease to be interested in him, so he turns back to the joys of boyhood. This time around, however, he has more money to spend, so he tends to buy the stamps he lusted for as a youth.

I have to admit I'm not a very conscientious or knowledgeable collector, but I do follow the hobby sporadically through stamp publications.

Last year Canada issued a stamp to commemorate the end of the Nazi Holocaust. It was a montage of snippets of German identity card photos of concentration camp prisoners. One was of Robert Engel, a German Jew who fled to the Netherlands, survived capture by the Gestapo, and was liberated from a Dutch transit camp by Canadian troops. Amazingly, John Prince, a stamp collector in Sarasota who went to school with Engel in Berlin in 1937, saw the stamp design in *Linn's Stamp News*, and recognized his old friend. The two men were reunited for the first time in fifty-nine years at a stamp show in Toronto.

"It is often said that stamp collecting brings people together," said Frank Baumann, who wrote the story. "Never before have I witnessed a demonstration of that truth as extraordinary, and as moving, as this one."

Astute networking can cover a lot of territory, including locating a long-lost friend who is a Holocaust survivor.

Unsolved Mysteries might be able to help.

So can astute networking.

MACKAY'S MAXIM
Even if you didn't go to USC, you can still take up stamp collecting.

Chapter 8

YOU KNOW WHO, BUT DOES WHO KNOW YOU?

Remember, the first strong impressions you make on someone else are the ones likely to end up as notes in their Rolodex.® And they're also the ones that are likely to stay there forever.

Obviously, you want to try for impressions that are both distinctive and positive. I know I've made the point earlier.

> *But never forget how important it is to do your homework and find out if you have some common ground when you know you're going to meet someone new.*

That's not prying. That's trying to establish a foundation for a relationship based on shared interests. You would do exactly the same thing if you were going on a date with someone you hadn't met before and wanted to make a favorable impression. (I know, I said that before too, but the dating angle is always a powerful way to reinforce the argument.)

How do you find out the information that will help you make that good impression?

Any way you can.

If the person is famous enough, check *Who's Who.*

If they're not? Call their office, get a bio, go to the library and check the index of the local newspaper, work your network; try to tap into theirs . . . In short, do whatever it takes to get the information you need.

MACKAY'S MAXIM

It does matter *how* they remember you, but it's more important that they *do* remember you.

Chapter 9

THE MOST IMPORTANT NETWORKING LESSON I EVER LEARNED

When I graduated from the University of Minnesota, I couldn't afford my own apartment. I lived at home in St. Paul. My mother had died just about the time I finished up at school, so my housemate was my father.

He was lonely.

I was trying to get my career started, and I was in over my head most of the time.

The result: a lot more father/son talks than I'd had in all the previous years we had lived together.

At the time, I was scratching out a living selling envelopes for Quality Park. I wanted to get on the fast track, but I didn't have a clue as to where the fast track was or how to catch the train that traveled on it.

My father did.

"Look, ever since you were seven years old, you've been batting golf balls around. I've seen you come in with bloody hands from hanging out at the driving range." (They gave me all the free whacks I wanted in exchange for running around in a golf cart with an iron cage mounted on it, picking up the loose balls.)

"Now that I think about it, golf is probably the only form of human activity you've taken seriously up to now.

Why don't you try to capitalize on what you do best?

"Go over to Minneapolis and pitch the admissions committee at the Oak Ridge Country Club. They're always buried in last place in the Minneapolis City Golf League. Tell them how you played golf for the University of Minnesota team, won the city championship twice, and was runner-up in the state high school tournament. They need new blood. They need talent. See if they'll let you in without having to pay the usual horrendous initiation fee, which neither of us can afford.

"If they do, you've got unlimited potential to make great business contacts. I think they have about 300 members, and most of them would love to play with you because of your low handicap. And maybe your generous and visionary employer will help you with the dues if you can show them some envelope action."

So why not? What's to lose in trying?

I gave the admissions committee the sales job of a lifetime. I figured the odds were the same as making a hole-in-one, but I gave it a shot.

"For nothing? You want us to admit you, a twenty-two-year-old kid, who knows virtually no one in the entire club, for nothing? Just so you can hustle our old duffers, pardon me, our distinguished members?"

Slight overswing. I had landed in a bunker.

"No, no, that isn't what I had in mind."

"Right. You want to help us win the City League Championship. Not sell envelopes."

"Well, not gamble on golf. I promise you I will never hustle a member. But I don't see anything wrong with making business contacts. That's what people do at country clubs. And just because I'm young, you shouldn't hold that against me. Young members are likely to pay dues for a lot more years than old members."

"No initiation fee?"

"I can't afford an initiation fee. Not now. Maybe someday."

"Someday? Then maybe we should defer your admission until someday."

"And blow off young members until they get old? And good golfers too?"

And so it went.

No sale. Triple bogey.

But I didn't throw away my clubs.

Six months and numerous meetings later, I was admitted.

For next to nothing down and a dues schedule I could live with, barely. As part of the deal, they made it clear they would be looking over my shoulder for any signs of improvement in my financial condition.

As I look back on my career, there's no question that this was the one single act that most helped me launch my career.

Three hundred members. Three hundred potential customers. Three hundred million unbet three-footers and Calcuttas. All in addition to the ton of new contacts in the city league.

What a network!

- Fingerhut Corporation—the huge direct mail company. My largest account forty years ago, and still my largest account today
- The Minnesota Vikings
- General Mills
- The Pillsbury Company
- Coast-to-Coast Stores
- Honeywell

To name just a few. So many new doors were opened up for me that within a few years I was top dog in sales at Quality Park and ready to go into business for myself.

But the best payoff was yet to come.

I was introduced to another former junior champ with a closet full of golf trophies.

Though my new golf partner never bought an envelope from me, she did say "I do." As a result, Carol Ann and I have been married for thirty-six years and raised three terrific kids together.

MACKAY'S MAXIM
Your best network will develop from what you do best.

Chapter 10

DOIN' WHAT COMES
UNNATURALLY

Fred was one of my schoolmates from fourth grade all through college.

He was a loner, a total introvert, painfully shy, with all the baggage that comes with it—the dead-fish handshake, the downcast eyes that never quite met yours, the halting, barely audible stabs at conversation.

Still, Fred was sincere, honest, hardworking, a thoroughly decent person.

I'm sure Fred went through high school without ever having a date. I can remember how, on graduation day, many of us trolled the halls to corral our classmates into signing our yearbooks. We competed with each other to see who could fill the most pages with reminiscences and tributes from their friends.

But not Fred. Once again, too timid, too shy. It would be a force job for Fred to go up to a classmate and request this easy favor.

Fast forward to college.

Somehow, Fred managed to get into a fraternity. Maybe it was because he never had a bad word to say about anyone. Maybe he was a "legacy." Maybe it was because Fred decided it was something he wanted badly enough to come out of his cocoon and really go for.

What was it that changed him? Only The Shadow knows.

Whatever it was, whatever it took, a new Fred began to emerge.

By our last year in college, he was unrecognizable from the Fred of our high school years.

He had become popular and gregarious. Fred's "lost years" in high school had not been entirely wasted. He seemed to know more about swing music and jazz than anyone else on campus, probably from listening to it alone in his room. He also developed a flair for dancing, a considerable social advantage.

After college, Fred and several of his fraternity brothers formed a partnership in the automotive business. They became very successful.

We all know people like Fred. Some of them never manage to shake off their early problems.

Others do.

For some people, networking is as natural and instinctive as breathing. We all know people who are self-confident, radiate optimism, make friends easily, and seem to glide through life on winged feet.

Not many of them will be readers of this book.

Why should they be? They do this stuff without even having to think about it. They network with their alarm clocks when they wake up in the morning.

This book—and particularly this chapter—is addressed to the rest of us, the Freds of the world, those not quite so sure of ourselves, perhaps a bit shy, even timid. We're not out there bowling over everyone we meet with our dazzling smiles or brilliant conversation. We're not even out there bowling.

For most people networking is a learned behavior, like learning to swim. It is a gradual—and often painful, even scary—process of trial and error, small incremental steps, and finally a few breakthroughs.

Fortunately, there are several tried and true techniques for overcoming this Fear of Trying.

1. Practice "let's pretend."

Why do we procrastinate? Why are we shy? We fear failure, and we define failure as falling short of perfection. Since perfection is impossible to achieve, we are conflicted and act tentatively, or don't act at all.

Plato said each thing or idea has a perfect form. While we can never achieve the ideal form, we should attempt to come as close as we can by observing and emulating the characteristics of the ideal.

Let's segue from the ancient Greeks to the modern angst-ridden networker. There is someone you want to meet. You have done your homework, you are aware of an affinity or a shared experience with this person, but you are afraid to make the first move.

Why not play a game with yourself? The name of the game is "Let's Pretend."

Ask yourself, "What would the ideal networker do in this situation?"

Pretend you are that person. And do it.

If you are able to do that, you can reinvent yourself.

By pretending you are what you are not, you actually can become what you have pretended to be.

2. Adopt a role model.

What's the difference between this suggestion and the Aristotle gambit?

Your ideal is real, not imagined.

You're not asking yourself what the perfect person would do, you've attached yourself to a successful networker and you're committed to studying his or her techniques.

In the best of all possible worlds, your role models also can become your mentors, helping you, advising you, guiding you, even lending you their network as you build your own.

For the shy or anxious person, this method has two advantages:

- It takes only one good connection to start you on your way.
- Your natural shyness and inexperience can help rather than hinder

you. As you gain confidence and skills, your role model will take pride in your progress and be motivated to do even more for you.

3. Take lessons.

You're taking one now, as you read this book, so you're already a believer in the learning process. There are other, real-life educational opportunities that are effective for overcoming shyness and inexperience.

The first real networking school I signed up for after I got out of college was Toastmasters. It proved so valuable to me that here I am many years later being paid handsomely as a public speaker, even though my main thrust is still running my business.

Toastmasters is not just about making speeches. It's about doing your homework, self-confidence, appearance, and becoming an interesting person and a valuable resource to others. In other words, Toastmasters can help you gain and polish the tools to become a successful networker.

The Dale Carnegie schools are designed to achieve similar goals. I'm a graduate, and I can tell you from my own experience that they are masters at instilling personal confidence, polish, poise, communication, and networking skills in their students. They've been around a long time—an excellent indication that they are getting results.

And if you hope one day to be a professional public speaker, or if you just want to sound like one, there is no better organization to join than the National Speakers Association (NSA), headquartered in Tempe, Arizona.

I am a member and collectively we speak to 20 million people a year. If you're looking to hire a speaker for an event, they're the ones to call. In fact, I believe this organization is so worthwhile that if you don't feel you got your money's worth the first year, send me a copy of your canceled check and I'll give you a "Harvey Mackay Scholarship"—the second year's membership is on me. NSA can be reached at (602) 968-2552 or via the Worldwide Web at www.NSASpeaker.org. They can explain to you about national membership and/or put you in touch with your local chapter.

4. Keep taking lessons.

Graduation is not the end of your education. It's the foundation, the launching pad, the beginning. Unless you keep your batteries charged, they will run down. For an ongoing source of inspiration and motivation, I recommend subscribing to Norman Vincent Peale's publication *Positive Living*. A similar publication in more condensed form is *Bits & Pieces*.

5. Join up.

Just about any group offers possibilities for making contacts and achieving personal growth: Dancing. Choir. Coin collecting. Horseback riding. Art appreciation. Theater going. Antique shopping. Politics. Great books. Wine. Food.

6. Have a little faith.

In yourself.

Dale Carnegie probably summed it up best: "You can make more friends in two months by becoming really interested in other people than you can in two years by trying to get other people interested in you. Which is just another way of saying that the way to make a friend is to be one."

MACKAY'S MAXIM

The more you exercise your networking muscles, the stronger they get—and the easier networking becomes.

START DIGGING!

Chapter 11

LOU HOLTZ'S NETWORKING STORY
How I Became a Coach

Introduction

As head coach of Notre Dame football for eleven years, Lou Holtz totally turned around the program he inherited.

In the five years immediately before he arrived, the Notre Dame won-lost record was 32 wins, 26 losses, 1 tie, and 2 bowl appearances.

The Holtz record, including his final 1996 season, was 100 wins, 30 losses, 2 ties, and 9 straight bowl appearances. It was so impressive that NBC took the unprecedented step of signing a separate deal with Notre Dame to televise all their home football games.

I helped recruit Lou as head coach at the University of Minnesota, his last stop before Notre Dame, and we've been close personal friends ever since. He currently serves on the Mackay Envelope Corporation Board of Directors.

The ultimate test of a coach's success is not just his won/lost record. That changes every week. What he instills in his players is what lasts a lifetime. Every week the Notre Dame locker room is filled with graduated players. They come back. The team is part of them. They are still part of the team.

Lou and I are constantly in touch. Before we part or before the phone call is ended, he will always say "Now, what can I do for you? How can I help you?"

I have taken him up on that offer time and again, and he has always delivered.

That's how I got this story.

Lou Holtz's Networking Story

There are many examples of how networking has helped me. One of the most important came early in my career. I wanted to coach for Woody Hayes at Ohio State, but I knew absolutely no one on his staff.

I didn't have a clue as to what to do until I mentioned my goal to Rick Forzano, a person whom I admired greatly and who was a football coach in the National Football League.

Rick knew exactly what to do. He arranged a meeting for me with Esco Sarkkinen, one of Hayes's assistants. I didn't realize it at the time, but Esco was sort of a gatekeeper for Woody. He kept a list of all the countless prospective candidates who wanted to join Woody's staff.

The meeting went well, but Esco was noncommittal and nothing happened. I decided not to let that discourage me. I stayed in touch with Esco as if I were a top candidate even though I didn't know if they were at all interested. I wrote him several times, kept him informed as to what I had been doing to keep myself prepared, and let him know that I continued to have a strong interest in being considered if any vacancy should arise.

The next year a miracle occurred. A vacancy opened up on the Ohio State coaching staff. Woody sat down with all his staff members, and they went around the room discussing the various candidates. Esco remembered me and was up to date on my activities and accomplishments over the past year. On his recommendation, I was interviewed for the position and subsequently hired at Ohio State by Woody Hayes. I was ecstatic.

I've thought about it a lot since because of the enormous impact it had on my career. There were many great candidates for the job, but I got it. I know it was because of my relationship with Rick, who could have written his own book on networking. (Sorry, Harvey.) And it was because I stayed in front of Esco during that long waiting period before the position opened up. When push came to shove, Esco had the ammunition he needed to fight for me. Without him in my corner, I would never have scored such a win at Ohio State, one of the most visible and successful football programs in the country.

> *As you can see, Lou hung in there and stayed with the game plan, even though the early results were not particularly encouraging.*

This experience taught Lou the value of getting to know as many people as possible in all kinds of different positions and to keep in touch.

In a word . . . networking.

MACKAY'S MAXIM

What do football and networking have in common? Without a well-thought-out game plan, you'll never score in the big game of life.

Chapter 12

WHAT IS A NETWORK?

For fifty years, the only companies we called "networks" were NBC, CBS, and ABC.

Now networking has been "discovered" in the true Hollywood sense. And it's not about the shelf life of news anymore. Networking has become the business buzzword of the '90s, from Netscape to the Internet.

Buzz. Buzz. Buzz.

But where's the beef?

A network provides a path, a way of getting from point A to point B in the shortest possible time over the least possible distance.

To expand on that a bit, it's finding first whom you need to get what you need in any given situation and then helping others do the same.

Networking is a way of connecting the dots between A and Z without having to go through C, D, E . . . W, X, and Y.

In other words, a network is geodesic rather than pyramidal. In a network, the interconnecting links can be lateral, vertical, or diagonal. Each link is no more or no less important than another. The whole structure is designed to minimize the distance between any one point and another. Each part reinforces the other.

My network is your network, my son's network is partially his mother's, whose network is in part our daughters', and so on, and so on, and so on . . .

You need to be open-minded and closed-mouthed in order to reap the benefits of building a geodesic network.

MACKAY'S MAXIM

A network is an organized collection of your personal contacts and your personal contacts' own networks. Networking is finding fast whom you need to get what you need in any given situation and helping others do the same.

Chapter 13

WHAT *ISN'T* A NETWORK?

One day a salesman driving on a two-lane country road got stuck in the ditch. He asked a farmer for help. The farmer hitched up Elmo, his blind mule, to the salesman's car. The farmer grabbed a switch, snapped it in the air, and yelled, "Go, Sam, go!" Nothing happened. He snapped it again. "Go, Jackson, go!" Still nothing. Then he flicked Elmo. "Go, Elmo, go!" And Elmo pulled the car out of the ditch.

"Hey, what's with the 'Sam' and the 'Jackson'?" asked the driver.

"Look, if he didn't think he had any help, he wouldn't even try!"

We all need help. Being part of a team is one way to get it.

But a network is different from a team.

Networking is not teamwork.

The easiest way to explain the distinction is to start way down the food chain.

An anthill is a marvelous example of teamwork. Each ant has a role to play, sometimes several roles. Some ants go out every morning and forage for leaves. Other ants digest the leaves and convert them into a kind of manna used to feed the entire colony. Others spend the day in the anthill, feeding and caring for the young or doing maintenance work. Still others groom and care for the queen ant. In some ant societies, there is even a standing army that specializes in raiding other colonies. They bring back prisoners to serve as slaves and perform menial chores. (Hey, this is sounding a lot like human society.)

An ant colony is a perfectly ordered, self-contained society. Every ant has its duties and performs them, without variation or complaint, until it dies. There are no better team players in nature.

But anthills are not networks.

No ant has ever put down his leaf, walked back to the nest, and said to another ant he happened to have grown up with, "Hey, buddy, I'm sick of spending every day carrying around ten times my own weight in leaves. And you must be bored to tears doing nothing but sweeping out the nest. Maybe it would be good for our morale if we rotated these jobs. What do you say that if I can arrange a little extra manna for you, we switch gigs?"

That would be networking, and ants do not network. They do what they do as part of the team and that's it.

Most corporations do not network. They are organized into tightly contained departments that function like silos. Information is accumulated vertically but never flows horizontally to other departments that might need it. R&D never talks to sales, sales never talks to customer service, and so on.

Orders go down the chain of command. Obedience comes up. The folks who work there are like ants; they're on automatic pilot.

Those organizations that do network, such as General Electric and 3M, are exceptions, and as a result, they are exceptionally successful. These companies try to break down the barriers between departments and the not-invented-here syndrome that goes with specialization and hierarchical systems.

They create cross-functional teams. They organize around serving customers instead of around serving themselves. They encourage individual initiative. They reward networking. They are not anthills.

Jack Welch, General Electric's CEO, is so determined to promote networking he has even invented his own networking buzzword: "boundarylessness."

"In business, what is worse than having departments?" asked Welch in *Fortune Adviser* in 1996. "They don't talk to each other. You have to make open behavior something that is rewarded. . . . Boundary-lessness says that every time you meet somebody you're looking for a better and newer and bigger idea. You are open to ideas from everywhere."

Unfortunately, most people do not network. When it comes to shaping their own careers and their own lives, they are team members, not individuals. They cut their leaves, sweep their nests, punch their clocks, and duck their heads.

So, look around. If the only people you're interacting with on a day-in, day-out basis are the other drones in your anthill, it's time to make some new connections.

MACKAY'S MAXIM

When was the last time you talked to someone outside your own department? If it has been longer than four hours, it has been too long.

Chapter 14

R.I.S.K. IT.
The Four Elements of Networking

You've heard what a network is and is not. Now you need to know the main ingredients that make a network tick. Remember them by the acronym R.I.S.K.—Reciprocity, Interdependency, Sharing, and Keeping at it.

Reciprocity

There's something we need to get straight right from the get-go. A network is not a love-in, it is a relationship formed to meet the needs of both parties on an ongoing basis. You give; you get. You no give; you no get.

While some networks are based on friendship, others are based on necessity. We network with friends and cronies because we like them. We network with others because they have something we need, and vice versa. The point is that if you only do business with people you like, you won't be in business very long.

Example

Vince was a big-city homicide cop. He'd had many years' experience as a uniformed street cop and a vice cop. Vince's network spanned three areas: informants, other cops, and judicial personnel—a category that included judges, attorneys, and court staff.

Vince solved more high-profile murder cases than any other cop in the history of his department. Was it good police work? Did he search for clues with a bigger magnifying glass?

Let Vince answer in true Vincean fashion: "I wouldn't know a clue if it bit me in the ass."

He freely admits he was no better than any other cop in analyzing a crime scene and figuring out whodunit.

"In fact, I wasn't as good as most of them."

I asked Vince how he had become such a legend in the department.

"I had the best network," he said. "Over the years, I developed a string of informants. Many were small-time grifters. I'd give them a break occasionally on some minor beef in exchange for information. One of my best networks was the parents of these guys. If sonny boy got in trouble, they wanted to help get him off the hook.

"But let me tell you about my best network of all. Years ago, when I was on the vice squad, one of my snitches, the desk clerk at a small downtown hotel, called me at home to tell me that several well-known hookers had drifted in and there seemed to be quite a bit of action going on in this particular suite of rooms. I got the key, and as was the practice in those days, I didn't knock, I simply opened the door and walked in. Imagine my surprise when I recognized all five of the johns.

"They were judges I had been dealing with for years.

" 'Sorry, fellows, I must have picked the wrong room,' I said, and closed the door.

"I never said another word about it to any of them, but from that moment on, believe me, I had five solid new members for my network. As time went by, the courts got pickier and pickier about granting warrants, but I never had a hard time finding a judge to sign a warrant for me.

"A lot of bad guys got put away because I burst into the wrong room."

Of course, Vince was something of a bad guy himself.

Networks are nice, but not everyone who has one is.

Vince has been able to push the "reciprocity" envelope to the limit.

In networking, reciprocity consists of the exchange of favors. The Vincean saga illustrates that favors come in many flavors, voluntary and involuntary, good and bad.

It also illustrates that while networking is effective, it is not always pretty.

Before you do a favor in business, it doesn't hurt to figure out first how the other person can repay you. He or she may not be able to pay off in dollars or advancement, for example, but can whisper the right words in the right places.

This doesn't have to be as cold-blooded as it sounds. You can have your network repay you by doing a favor for a third party. For instance, let's say you took a role in a local charity drive as a favor to a member of your network who is an advertising executive. He owes you. Recently, a third person, another member of your network, someone *you* owe, asked you to find her kid a summer internship with a company that does creative work. Hmmm. I think I know who I'd call.

Positive Networking Favors You May Rely on in Just About Any Business

- Helping other people prepare for a major presentation they must make by: coaching them, critiqueing them, and acting as their sounding board. Do these things with gusto, no matter how boring the topic may be.
- Formally and frankly thanking people for their sincere help, even when their help fails to be of benefit. They still made the effort.
- Helping to develop a subordinate (especially one in another department) through counseling or encouragement and without the expectation of a thank-you in return.
- Giving colleagues in another department a "heads-up" about bad news in a report that affects them or a tip-off about a "surprise" visit by top brass rather than sitting back and gloating that other guys are about to get nailed.
- Doing someone else's dirty work for them, when the dirty work is

thankless drudgery like completing the monthly sales report and the help is completely unexpected and at a time when the other person is snowed with work. Basically, help the other person, whether he's on your level or she's in a senior position.

Negative Networking Consists of:

- Sharing gossip or inside information about other people that you have learned in confidence. It doesn't take long for people to figure out where the stab in the back came from, and they are likely to retaliate. But the worse damage will be to your reputation if you become known as a back-stabber or a gossip.
- Shuffling an incompetent person between departments just to protect his or her job. This is unfair and unproductive to both the person and the organization.
- Agreeing with your competitors to fix prices or to exchange trade secrets to keep out a new competitor. This one can get you sent to the Charlie Ward suite at Greystone College.
- Doing other people's dirty work for them when the dirty work involves violating federal laws (like those governing sex or age discrimination, product safety, truth in advertising, etc.). Result? See preceding entry.

Interdependency

One of the myths of modern business is that corporations can establish formal business structures that define the limits of these networks. For instance, every chain of fast-food restaurants has a corps of managers. All managers share certain responsibilities for performing and reporting. From time to time the company will bring them together for training or to inform them about new corporate policies.

It's the old anthill syndrome all over again. Here's your manual. This is how it's done. Period.

However, these are non-ants we're talking about here. In the process of getting to know each other, they're also going to bond, not necessarily in ways the company anticipated.

Let me give you an example of how it works.

Curt Carlson is the head of the Carlson Companies. Curt is the only eighty-year-old I know who still works twelve-hour days. He is also the only billionaire I know.

One day I made plans to meet Curt and his wife, Arleen, in the lobby of the Radisson Hotel in Scottsdale. He owns the Radisson chain. A big four-color picture of Curt, dressed in a snappy blue suit and red tie, hangs in every hotel and restaurant he owns.

Curt definitely had dressed down for this occasion, no doubt to make it less likely he would be recognized by the help. Arleen was not with the incognito program. She looked like a million or, rather, a billion dollars.

"Where are we going to lunch?" I asked.

"How about T.G.I. Friday's?" he said. He owns that chain too.

"There's one about six blocks away," I replied.

"Nah, I ate there yesterday."

"I don't know where there's another one nearby."

"We'll ask the bell captain," said Curt.

We ambled over to the bellhop station.

"Is there another T.G.I. Friday's anywhere around other than the one just down the road?" he inquired.

"In Mesa."

"How far is that?"

"About a thirty-minute drive," he said, "but you know, the best food in town is right here at the hotel."

"Thanks," said Curt. He pressed a bill into the bellhop's hand. "Glad you feel that way about this place, but we're going to Mesa."

With Harvey as the wheel man, of course.

When we got there, the place was jammed. Somehow, the hostess found us a nice table.

"Would you send the manager over, please?" asked Curt.

"Certainly, sir," she said.

Two minutes later she was back.

"The manager wanted you to know he will be over in just a few minutes."

Hurumph.

Another few minutes and she was back again.

"It will be just a minute or two more. Please excuse him for the delay. He will be over just as soon as possible."

Hurumph. Hurumph.

Eventually a young man in a neatly pressed blue suit and a red tie emerged.

"I'm the manager. How can I be of service?"

"I'm Curt Carlson."

"Why, sir, what a wonderful surprise. We're truly honored to have you here."

"And this is my wife, Arleen, and this is Harvey Mackay."

"Oh, yes, Mr. Mackay. I've read all your books." (Did I mention how exceptionally good the food is at the Mesa T.G.I. Friday's?)

"Sit down," said Curt, who began peppering him with questions about gross receipts, average check per person, all the minutiae of the restaurant game. The manager had every answer to the penny.

"I don't see many students here," said Curt. The restaurant was right in the middle of the Mesa Community College campus.

"That's right, sir. They'd like to come, but they're usually on pretty tight budgets, so you won't see them very much unless they come with their folks. But they know we're here, and that's the important thing because we'll get them as regulars a few years from now when they come back with their own families."

Curt beamed.

On the way back to Phoenix, I asked him what he thought about the meeting with the manager.

"I give him high marks. I give the Friday's manager in Scottsdale high marks. I give the bell captain at the Radisson high marks," said Curt. "And I give myself low marks."

"Why is that?"

"Because this Prince and the Pauper routine isn't working. After I pulled it yesterday at lunch, I'm sure the Scottsdale manager was on the phone to all his fellow managers within one hundred miles telling them to be on the lookout for me, and I'd bet the bell captain called Mesa as soon as we were out the door."

"So why did it take the manager ten minutes to get over to the table today?"

"Because he was checking his numbers and spiffing up. Wouldn't you? There's one thing I don't understand though," said Curt.

"What's that?" I asked.

"How the hell did he know who you were?"

That's Curt.

Sharing

Have you heard about the meticulous spender? He's the guy with the little black book, who wrote down every nickel he ever spent but never stopped to add it up.

Some so-called networks are designed the same way. They have plenty of information but their systems are not designed to use it.

For instance, highly structured companies tend to filter information upward through layers of management until the news reaches the top. When it does, every department has to put its stamp on it, and it's distorted and out of date.

Remember the old parlor game where ten people stand around in a circle and the first one whispers a bit of gossip in the second person's ear and the second person passes it on to the third and so on until it reaches the first person again, invariably in an unrecognizable form?

Sharing is the element of networking that is meant to avoid that kind of breakdown. It does that by slicing away layers of bureaucracy and time delays and getting the information around as quickly and clearly as possible so it can be acted on by people who know how to use it.

Ironically, the kinds of organizations that look so neat and orderly on wall charts, like military organizations, are exactly the kinds that are anti-network. When a sergeant in vehicle maintenance can't talk to a sergeant in procurement about bad replacement fuel pumps without going up the ladder to his lieutenant, who then reports to the captain, who then sends a memo to the maintenance major, who then reaches across to the procurement major, who sends word back down the ladder to the procurement sergeant, the organization is not deeply into the sharing thing.

Strange as it seems, often the messier the organization, the better the kind of sharing that generates good results. But hey, think of sharing like bad news. Nothing travels faster or over a more twisted route.

3M's networking style is a prime example of the right approach. It's been described as "managed chaos" where new employees are pushed to learn about 3M's simultaneously nourishing and ruthless environment via a class in risk taking. They attend with their supervisors and are taught . . . to be willing to defy their supervisors. They hear stories about victories won despite the opposition of the boss—like how Livio DeSimone (3M's chairman and CEO) five times tried and failed to kill the project that became the wildly successful Thinsulate—to hammer home the importance of fighting hierarchical structure to champion winning ideas.

Is it any wonder that just about every year 3M is among the top ten in *Fortune*'s list of the most admired companies?

Like 3M, "boundarylessness" at General Electric under Jack Welch is heavily into the sharing principle.

A recent article in *The New York Times* describes a new breed of executive, so new they've just invented a name for them, the CLO, or Corporate Learning Officer. Their job? "Encouraging employees to share knowledge—letting the right hand know what the left hand is doing. The growth of information and the often huge size of companies make the task difficult, and because the stakes are high, a growing number of corporations—including Coca-Cola, Cigna, EDS, Hewlett-Packard, Monsanto, U.S. West, and Young & Rubicam—are hiring CLOs and paying them salaries between $300,000 and $700,000."

Are they worth it?

Monsanto learned—the hard way—that they are.

A Monsanto salesman had heard rumors that a big sale the com-

pany was competing for was in trouble, but no network existed for him to get word back to the right people as to how to get the sale back on track. Monsanto lost a million-dollar sale.

As a result, Monsanto is building a "knowledge management architecture," which includes an internal, on-line news and information network to avoid just these kinds of communication foul-ups.

Saving one large customer a year probably will pay for the whole system.

At General Electric, sales of "white goods"—big-ticket appliances—were in the deep freeze. The boss called a meeting to discuss what he assumed was a marketing or advertising problem. Fortunately, GE is GE, so there's always a lot of true networking going on between departments, and a representative of GE Capital was present. He pulled out a chart showing that consumers were up to their eyeballs in debt.

"Suddenly everyone had a whole new angle on the problem," said Steven Kerr, the GE version of a CLO.

The information called for a financial, rather than a marketing, solution, such as stretching out payments to make it easier for consumers to pay for the products.

So here we have two fairly typical business problems. The solutions were based on getting the right information to the right people at the right time. The means of achieving those solutions was networking.

Is it worth big bucks to put an internal, informal company network into operation?

GE thought so, and it paid off.

Monsanto didn't, but they do now.

Keeping at It

If your network is going to work, you have to stay plugged in and keep the wires humming.

When I decided to write my first book, my writing experience was limited to a few articles in regional magazines. I had a lot of ideas, but

I didn't have clue one about how to organize them into a readable format, let alone how to find anyone to publish them.

After a lot of digging, I realized there were a number of people who could provide me with the help I needed. I'd had no close contact with many of them for decades, but I'd stayed in touch with them by systematically working my way through my Rolodex year after year, birthday and holiday after birthday and holiday. Those lines may have gotten a little frayed, but I never let them break. While we might not have seen each other in years, we'd kept up on each other's lives through family letters, short notes, and the occasional fuzzy photograph.

One of those lines connected with a proverbial high school nerd turned success story. In the years since we were in Mr. Ford's chemistry class together, I doubted if I would ever have much contact with Dale again. He was your quintessential grind, not big on the social circuit. We were lab partners, and even though I couldn't tell you the formula for water and he was a giant in the Science Club, we liked each other. We had our moments, like the time we dropped ice down the backs of each other's shirt.

Since graduation, I had probably seen him only four or five times, but we kept up the Christmas cards, and I enjoyed sending and receiving an annual update. Thirty-five years later, I found myself in the role of a first-time author trying to peddle a book with a weird-sounding title against huge odds. My circle of business acquaintances consisted largely of envelope gamers, not exactly the traditional launching pad for literary endeavors, but there was Dale's name jumping out at me from my Rolodex.

I noted that he had gone into something related to the book business. A wholesaler? What's that? Why would anyone need that kind of service? It turned out that everyone—every book retailer, anyway—did need someone who did just that, and Dale had become the biggest book wholesaler on the West Coast.

I called him. When he figured out who was on the phone, he said he checked to see if something had been dropped down the back of his shirt again. And then he ordered 10,000 books, ten times the usual number. After I thanked him, he said, "I didn't have a lot of fun in

high school, but I've always remembered our friendship and how much I enjoyed it. It's meant a lot to me."

Reciprocity

Interdependency

Sharing

Keeping at it

Remember them by the letters "R.I.S.K." The only risk is to not use them.

> **M A C K A Y ' S   M A X I M**
> The really big networking mistakes people make in their lives come from the risks they never take.

Chapter 15

SIXTEEN CORNERSTONES FOR A SOLID NETWORK

~

I f you ever have to make one of those infamous 2 A.M. phone calls, if it isn't the doctor, chances are it's going to be to one of the people in the categories described here.

Here's my choice of the sixteen most likely candidates. If I get any mail at all from readers of this book, my guess is it's likely to be about this list.

"Why didn't you have plumbers?"

"What about a psychiatrist?"

"Shouldn't everyone know a first-rate electrician?"

Yeah, they're all in my list of "Thirty Cornerstones for a Solid Network." Or maybe it's fifty. Whatever. You draw the line. This is just a starting place. (But say, I really could use the name of a good plumber. Every time it rains here, the basement floods.)

1. Real estate broker

If you're an average American, you'll buy and sell six houses in the course of a lifetime.

That's twelve transactions, each one of which may represent, in dollar terms, the biggest deal you will ever make.

It will pay you many times over to have someone on your side who

knows the business and the local market and is personally loyal to you and your interests.

Make a real estate agent a key member of your network. Today, in most states, real estate agents will agree to represent your interests, whether you are a buyer or a seller. Historically, this was not the case. The agent always worked on behalf of the seller, not the buyer. Therefore, the agent's loyalty—and legal obligation—was to represent the seller's interests.

Many buyers were not aware of this and thought real estate agents automatically represented their interests. In some states, buyers have sued and won, charging that the agent misled them. Agents now tend to be up front with buyers and disclose their true affiliation from the get-go. Most states require it.

If you're a buyer, that should serve as an early warning signal. Make sure you get a real estate agent on your team!

You need someone just as experienced, just as market savvy, just as knowledgeable as the seller has.

You need your own real estate agent.

If you have previously been a seller and you are satisfied with the result, ask the real estate agent who represented you then to represent you now as a buyer.

The agent's fee is usually a percentage that comes out of the purchase price paid to the seller. But you can offer to pay the agent instead. If you're worried that your agent might encourage you to buy a more expensive home to earn a higher percentage commission, offer to pay a fixed amount for his or her services.

What if you have never been a seller previously, or you're looking in a new area?

That's what a network is for.

When Carol Ann and I decided to buy a vacation home in Phoenix, we were complete strangers to the community. Left on our own, someone could have sold us beachfront property on the Grand Canyon, and we'd still be waiting for the tide to come in. We needed someone who knew the territory. I used my Young Presidents Organization network to recommend a real estate agent.

Our agent earned her fee five times over. In the first eighteen months after we bought our home, the value appreciated 35 percent. In addition, our agent found us a banking connection and a real estate lawyer to handle the transaction. Most important, she introduced us to her network in the community. We're as much at home here as if we'd landed in the middle of a Minnesota snowdrift.

When it comes to thinking about a new home, think about movers too. Movers can be shakers. They can be as instrumental as real estate agents in reducing grief—or inflicting pain.

2. Source for hard-to-get tickets

Your best customer just called. The Bulls are in town. Tonight. He needs four tickets. Courtside. Well, what are you going to do?
1. Tell him to take his business some place else?
2. Tell him you don't know how to get tickets?
3. Tell him you'll try and then go down to the stadium in −3 degree weather and try to connect with a seller and try to figure out where the seats he's trying to sell you are located, and try to get back to your customer in time to let him know what, if anything, you've been able to do. (By the way, this is one time you can leave home without your American Express card. Bring cash. Lots and lots of cash.)
4. Tell him you'll take care of it, call your ticket connection, and have the tickets delivered to your customer?

The correct answer is (4), unless you're planning on early retirement.

The fact is, there is no such thing as a sold-out house. Money will get you honey. But you have to know who to ask.

I've found last-minute tickets to everything from the U.S. Open to the Olympics. And not always at scalpers' prices either. I don't rely on any one person but a network (there's that word again) of people I've cultivated over the years. Who?
- Concierge
- Promoters/sponsors for the event
- Coaches/players/staff/owners
- Media
- Ticket brokers (listed every day in *USA Today*)

■ Publishers (Yes, contact my publisher. Call Doubleday in New York and ask for Harriet. Ask her to get you tickets to Broadway shows. She'll be delighted. Won't you, Harriet?)

3. Travel Agent

For every one hundred people on an airplane, there are one hundred different ticket deals. How can you afford not to have a resourceful travel agent?

4. Catholic/Jewish/Protestant/African American/Feminist community leader . . . just to name a few

These days you can get in trouble with any identifiable group without even hardly trying, but if you have an ally within that group who will speak out on your behalf, you'll have a basis for defending yourself against any unfair charges.

If you want a global, culturally diversified powerhouse for your workforce, your board, or your network, here's the perfect source.

Buy tickets to the annual dinner. Run an ad in the program. Hire. Help. Support. Recognize. Network. Network. Network.

5. Headhunter

Most people don't talk to headhunters until they need a job. That's a move that needlessly short-changes their network. Don't hang up the next time a headhunter calls, no matter how happy you are in your present job. Say something like "I'm not really interested, but I'm flattered you'd call. In fact, from time to time, we may want to use your talents to locate qualified people. Let me have your phone number, and maybe in a couple of months, we can have lunch and get to know each other a little better."

What have you just done? Well, you've turned the conversation around to your advantage. While stating how content you are with your present situation, you've also kept the lines of communication open. You have begun to lay the foundation for a relationship.

If you had been so desperate to find a new job that, in response to an anonymous voice on the phone, you had indicated you were unhappy with your present situation and jumped at the chance for a meeting, the headhunter would have thought less of you—and your value would have been marked down accordingly.

Headhunters tend to be pretty sophisticated at reading between the lines. They know the "we-may-be-looking-for-help" line is just a way of keeping the lines open. But you can be sure they'll call you back, and you can meet with them or not. At least you now know where to find someone who can help you find a new job before you need one.

Okay, no headhunter has ever called and you want to meet one? Call one up, use the "we-may-be-looking-for-someone" line, so you have a cover, and get started.

Headhunters will know what you really have in mind, but so what? They don't care. These are long-term relationships, and this is really a case where it pays to dig your well before you're thirsty, because you don't want to have to begin one of these relationships when you're already heading out the door.

6. Banker

As with headhunters, most people don't hang out with their bankers until they're being hung out to dry, usually in the form of financial problems. Bad idea.

7. Elected local official

Unless you're seeking a presidential pardon or appointment to the federal judiciary, you're better off knowing your local council member than you are knowing the president.

What can City Hall types do for you?

Damn near everything: get your snow-filled street plowed; fill the potholes; pick up the garbage; fix the sidewalks; trim the trees; lower your property tax bill; get your zoning changed; deal with nuisance neighbors; regulate neighborhood businesses; catch stray animals; enact ordinances; monitor air, water, and noise quality; enforce antidis-crimination legislation.

Among other things.

What they can't and won't do is get your kid a summer job on the street crew.

And they're so accessible and easy to please! All it takes is time and little money. Try talking to a U.S. Senator on the telephone. Once in a lifetime. Try talking to a live human being at your local public utility on the phone. Not in this lifetime. Now try your council member. Chances are you will make real human contact within the working day.

It won't hurt those chances if you're a supporter. And it also won't hurt if you are representing a potential block of voters, such as your neighborhood association or all the businesses down in the local office park.

8. High-ranking cop

No, not for fixing tickets. That's tacky. Do you ever go out of town and leave the house unoccupied? You want to be sure a patrol drives by the place at frequent intervals. Ever need to know who belongs to a certain license number? Ever have a noisy neighbor you don't care to confront directly? Ever want to know more about the kids your kids are hanging around with? Who you gonna call?

9. Firefighters

You want to be sure the locals responsible for covering your home/business know where you live and will give a call to your residence priority. A little remembrance at Christmas will help them remember you the rest of the year.

10. Celebrity

Why? Because many of these people are rentable for golf foursomes or other social events, and they can be invaluable chips in negotiating situations.

The late Steve Ross clawed his way from a thread-bare Depression boyhood in Brooklyn to the top of the heap as the head of Time Warner. He was a legendary dealmaker.

In *Master of the Game*, Connie Bruck describes a tough negotiation in which Ross was competing with another company to buy Atari. Ross sent the corporate jet to San Jose to pick up the sellers for a meeting in New York City. When they boarded the plane, Clint Eastwood and his then-partner, actress Sondra Locke, were on board. Apologizing profusely for any intrusion, the pilot explained that the plane would have to make another stop to let the movie stars off at a location where they would be filming. The star-struck sellers didn't mind a bit. In fact, they wound up selling Atari to Ross on terms far more favorable than they originally had intended.

Seduction of the innocent was Ross's trademark negotiating technique. He could overwhelm the most jaded Hollywood types with extravagant gestures, like sending the corporate jet cross-country to pick up Steven Spielberg's dogs so they could join the director on a weekend getaway.

I have my own Ross story. I played tennis with him at the John Gardiner Tennis Ranch in Phoenix. We were playing doubles and spun the racquet for partners. Ross got a partner he didn't want.

"Two out of three," Ross said, turning on his famous million-dollar grin. With the not-so-innocent, it was take what you can get.

How do you meet celebrities?

Hey, it's lonely at the top. A lot of celebrities are more accessible than you might think.

Everyone—including celebrities—has lawyers, doctors, dentists, accountants, relatives, favorite restaurants, and hangouts.

And celebrities also have agents, promoters, public relations specialists, and coaches.

Use the old *Six Degrees of Separation* gambit and get friendly with someone who knows the someone you want to know. Then ask that someone to arrange a meeting for you, or at least make the first call on your behalf. If I get a phone call from someone who says "Joe Blow told me to call," and Joe hasn't called me first, I know that this person can't be all that important to old Joe. As a result, that person doesn't become a priority for me.

The first celebrities I ever met were golfers. I played golf in college, loved to follow the pros, and was a face in the crowd whenever a tournament came to town. If I couldn't get the promoter, some bigwig at the country club, or the golf pro to give me an introduction, I'd simply hang around until the right moment came and then stick out my mitt and say how glad I was to meet them. If I was permitted to babble on long enough, I usually got in a few reasonably coherent words about the game and my knowledge of the golfers' own achievements. Once or twice I was able to connect well enough to eventually form a first-name-basis friendship.

Yes, it takes a certain amount of brass, but if you do your homework—that is, if you learn something about the person you want to meet and their interests—you have a good chance of hitting it off.

11. Veterinarian

It isn't your life or your death, but anyone who ever lost a pet because of less than first-rate emergency care will feel almost as badly as if it were.

12. Insurance expert

Sure, you can wait until Monday morning to find out if you're covered. Do you really want to? And would you like to discover you aren't covered because you didn't buy the right policy? You can skip this one if the possibility of eking out your twilight years on your social security pension doesn't bother you.

13. Divorce lawyer

Why not criminal defense attorney? You don't have to search very hard to find out who the stars are in this area, because the names of the town's leading criminal lawyers appear in the papers with sad regularity. Besides, the chances of your needing one are rather remote.

On the other hand, remember the "50-50" rule: 50 percent of all marriages end in divorce, and 50 percent of your assets can wind up on the table.

Also remember the conventional wisdom: The largest single investment you'll ever make in your life is your house. Well, not if you get divorced it isn't. Then it's a scrap of paper titled Final Decree.

What a divorce lawyer and a criminal lawyer have in common is that, unlike other lawyers, when you need one, hey, you really need one. Now. Does it make sense to turn your life over to some name you pick out of the phone book?

No. That's why you check out the legal talent in this area far in advance of having to check into that room at the Y.

(No, Carol Ann, I don't really know any divorce lawyers. This is one time I haven't taken my own advice.)

14. Auto mechanic

A good, honest auto mechanic is worth his weight in gold because a bad, dishonest one will cost you his weight in gold.

15. Media contact

Take it from a reporter's son, even if you use this contact only once in a lifetime, it can save you from a world of pain.

Here's the scenario: A reporter calls you out of the blue and confronts you with some exceedingly negative rumor—something you definitely don't want to see on the 10 P.M. news. Will your media buddy save you from this embarrassment? Probably not. Princes and presidents have to see and read this stuff about themselves, so you won't escape totally unscathed either.

But your media contact represents your single best shot at getting your own spin on the story. Real PR pros can help here too. They do this for a living.

However, what you really need is an insider who will go to bat for you. Tough assignment, but a great addition to any network.

How do you add these people to your network? By being a reliable source. Give them what they need and they may—*may*—give you what you need.

16. Best friend

Most important of all. The one person in the world you can tell *anything* to.

MACKAY'S MAXIM

People aren't strangers if you've already met them. The trick is to meet them *before* you need their help.

Chapter 16

NETWORK AS IF YOUR LIFE DEPENDED ON IT, BECAUSE IT DOES

How do you buy a car?

If you're a careful and prudent shopper, you research one or more respected consumer publications to learn which makes and models represent the best quality and value; you consult your network; you consider your own prior experiences with various cars.

Then you comparison-shop, weighing various factors such as price, service, convenience, reputation, selection.

Finally, you bargain vigorously and drive off proudly in your new purchase, convinced that you have done all that is humanly possible to get yourself the most suitable vehicle at the best possible price.

How do you buy an operation?

You do what your doctor tells you.

In other words, when it comes to saving a few bucks on a car, you'll move heaven and earth to make the best deal. But when it comes to saving your life, you take whatever solution is recommended to you by the first person you talk to.

Hmmm.

Now I'm not one to say that doctors are not honest and capable.

But folks, people are people.

Some doctors are better than others.

Bad car deals can cost you money. Bad docs can cost you your life.

A year ago, I learned that Sam, one of our manufacturing employees, was about to have prostate surgery. This is a rather sensitive subject with most men, but I felt compelled to discuss it with him. I'm no stranger to this situation. Neither are a lot of other guys. Prostate cancer has been the number-two killer in men since time immemorial. Each year 34,000 American males die from it. I had prostate surgery five years ago. Since then I've never delivered a speech without warning men over age fifty that they *must* get a PSA test annually.

It was not a dry-eyed meeting, even though Sam told me he had passed the bone scan—the test that determines whether the cancer had spread.

Naturally, he was worried about his family and, of course, his own survival.

Unlike many men, who were too embarrassed to get examined, Sam had been smart. He'd been checked at frequent intervals, had the PSA test, and as a result, he'd been diagnosed in the early stages. I assured him that the odds were greatly in his favor. (Believe me, I had done my homework when I was in his shoes.)

I told him that just nine days after the surgery I'd been able to walk five miles and that I was back to my five- to seven-mile running groove in six weeks.

No, the surgery was not exactly a trip to Disneyworld, but you can take any amount of pain just as long as you know (1) it's going to end and (2) the price you pay is worth the result.

Next question—mine—and the answer was just as critical as the bone scan results.

"Who's your doctor?"

"Doctor X."

"Okay, do you want me to check him out?"

From the astonished look on his face, I could see that this idea was not programmed on Sam's disk. Sam was a good envelope guy. He might spend a week checking out the specs on a $100,000 sorting machine for the company, but with his life on the line, it hadn't occurred to him to check out the person responsible for working the on-off switch on himself.

Why was this important? Not just because Sam wanted every trace of the cancer removed. One slip and Sam has incontinence problems—or sexual dysfunction—and all the baggage that could go with it. Sam had to make sure Dr. X was on the cutting edge.

"Sure, check him out," Sam said.

So I did.

With a few phone calls, I got back a very average report card. Not the kind of review I'd accept on anyone I was about to hire to make envelopes, much less perform surgery on my bod.

Next day I gave Sam the news, suggested he find a new surgeon, and offered a few names—his call, of course.

The bottom line? Sam chose a new doctor—in fact, the same doctor who had performed my surgery.

He's back at work and there has been no trace of the cancer since the operation.

There is no consumer publication that will tell which doctor is good and which isn't. Oh yes, there are several "Best Doctor"–type books and magazine articles around, but that's not the route I'd take.

A piece of paper can't talk back to you or answer questions. A customer can.

For sure, the great business-getters will be in these books and articles. The docs who have great referral relationships with other docs will be there. The docs who know how to schmooze with the media will be there. In other words, the best networkers will be in there. But the best networkers do not necessarily make the best docs.

If you want to find the best doc, you gotta ask.

If your doctor tells you, "They're all the same," then it's time to get a new doctor.

People, including doctors, manifestly, are not *all* the same.

If the doctor gives you a name and tells you that is the best, then unless he, she, or a member of their immediate family has been actually treated by this same doctor, it's "Thanks, Doc, I'll keep it in mind."

Would you ask the owner of the restaurant you're eating in for the name of the best restaurant in town?

Would you ask a car dealer for the name of the best car dealer in town?

That's why you don't rely on the doc.

There's an old—and all too true—joke. What do you call the person who graduated last in his medical school class?

Doctor.

Is that the person you want operating on you?

If you want the best, you check with the carvees, not the carvers.

Which ones?

The people who would engage the services of the best doctor in town and only the best doctor in town.

Who would those people be?

They would tend to be the best, the most successful, the most prominent in their own fields.

The best (<u>fill in the blank</u>) in town isn't going to get operated on by some kid just out of medical school. He or she is going to get the best there is.

> *Go with the best to find the best.*

And if you're not content to go with the best in town, and you want the best in the world, come on up to Minnesota and go to the Mayo Clinic, where Ronald Reagan, Muhammad Ali, Barbara Bush, King Hussein, Arnold Palmer, and many of the most prominent people on Earth go for treatment.

Before you decide I'm just rooting for the hometown team, read this.

An article buried in a newspaper recently described a Mayo Clinic patient named Sheik Zayid bin Sultan Al Nuhayyan, president of the United Arab Emirates. The sheik spent a month at Mayo, where he had neck surgery.

The headline read: "Sheik leaves state—with a few souvenirs."

The sheik—and an entourage of 140—left Rochester International Airport yesterday with about 18 truckloads of goods, including furniture bought in Minneapolis and items from Dayton's in Rochester. Their purchases were loaded into a separate cargo plane, which took off earlier Wednesday.

The sheik—one of the wealthiest men in the world—and his entourage had occupied more than 100 rooms in local hotels, and the visit apparently produced a windfall for several downtown re-tailers, limousine services and other businesses.

Do you think the sheik would have settled for less than the best, even if he had to fly halfway across the world to get it?

If you're smart, there are three wells you'll be sure to dig before you're thirsty.

One is labeled "Best Doctors."

One is labeled "Best Lawyers." (This is in addition to the best divorce lawyers whom we have already talked about.)

One is labeled "Best Accountants."

They may not be easy to find.

So what?

Here's how you do it, paint-by-the-numbers style.

Doctor

At this point, you're new in town and looking for an internist, a general family practitioner.

If there's a teaching hospital in your new town, the head of the internal medicine department at that teaching hospital is the best GP in town. This is the doc who runs the program that trains other docs to go out into the world and heal the sick.

If there is a lord of life and death on Earth in human form, this person is it. And he knows it. So he will not be an easy person to arrange a meeting with. And he probably does not take private patients either.

Whatever.

Six Degrees of Separation. Somehow get in to see him. Tell him that you know that, by virtue of his position, he is uniquely qualified both as a doctor and as a teacher of doctors to make a recommendation.

Ask him for one.

He won't give it to you.

Yes, he knows the answer to your question.

Doesn't matter. He still won't give it to you.

He doesn't want to pick and choose from among the hundreds of people he's trained. He loves them all. They are his students, his gift to the world, his legacy. But, as in every family, some are more talented than others.

The key is to phrase your question in such a way that he knows you will not embarrass him or compromise his position.

Tricky stuff.

If you're really gutsy, you might ask him who his doctor is.

Whatever you ask, you're not likely to get a straight answer, but listen carefully anyway. He might refer you to someone who will refer you to someone else.

Whatever he tells you, if there are some names attached to it, even if they aren't docs, follow up.

And of course, when you do, make sure the person you're referred to knows who did the referring.

Okay, you're not in a city with a teaching hospital. The first thing to do is to call up your doc in your last town and ask if she knows anyone who knows the name of the best GP in your new town. No one will give you a single name in this scenario either. You're a civilian and this fraternity/sorority is so closed off to civilians, it makes Skull & Bones look about as exclusive as Sam's Club.

Don't ask her to write you. Ask her to call you back, so you can ask some questions—and she can speak more freely. Where did the doc go to school? What kind of practice? What type of patients does this doc tend to attract? How long in practice? What hospital affiliation? What is the reputation of the hospital? What makes her so good?

At best, you'll get a couple of names, but it's a start.

Next step, ask whoever hired you or whoever is your new boss for the name of their doc. Or the name of the company president's doc.

If you already have a lawyer, ask your lawyer for the name of his or her doctor. (But not if it's personal injury lawyer. The doc and the lawyer might, in effect, be in business with each other.)

Accountant? Same.

Try your names out on a few other people, particularly fussy people and people who can afford the best care. Get their doc's names.

Cross-check. By this time, the same couple of names should be popping up.

You're as close as you're going to get.

Make a choice.

You've got your doc.

Or you could just go down to the Mayo Clinic and ask for the name of the doc who treated Sheik Zayid bin Sultan Al Nuhayyan.

Lawyer

What do you need in the way of legal work? Estates. Torts. Real estate. Contracts. Employment. Corporate. Tax. You need all of it. No lawyer does all of it anymore or is good at all of it anymore.

You need a law firm. A law firm that does it all. This is easier than the doc thing, since you can generally judge the quality of the law firm by the quality of the clients, and it's a lot easier to get the names of a law firm's clients than a doc's clients.

Martindale & Hubbell publishes a national directory of leading law firms that lists both the names of the lawyers and their largest and most prestigious clients. The book can be found in any public library.

If there are large, important corporations around town, the law firms that work for them tend to be quite competent in the areas I've listed. These firms usually service not only their corporate clients' needs but also the personal legal needs of the corporation's key executives (who sometimes, miraculously, pay much lower fees than the going rate for their personal work. Could that have anything to do with where they steer the corporate business?). Since these law firms' personal clientele tends to be bright, affluent, sophisticated, and lead complicated lives, the lawyers at these firms are also high-caliber professionals.

But that doesn't mean you should go to the same firm that your company uses.

The opposite is true: Do *not* use the same law firm as your employer. Hey, didn't I just say that's where most firm's big execs go? Yep. And it's a mistake. Too many potential conflicts of interests. Too much knowledge of your personal affairs floating around the office.

Lawyers take a vow of confidentiality? Oh, yeah, so do doctors, clergy, newspapers, and Heidi Fleiss. But people are people. Things slip out.

Get your personal attorney elsewhere. Another large firm with a prestigious corporate clientele will do nicely for most of your work. However, don't use it for divorce work or criminal work. These tend to be the weakest departments in white-shoe law firms. Go to the specialists.

Accountants

Let's make it easy for a change. You can't go wrong with one of the Big Six: Arthur Andersen, Deloitte & Touche, KPMG Peat Marwick, Price Waterhouse, Coopers & Lybrand, Ernst & Young. These firms do accounting work for the nation's major corporations and also take individuals. They hire only the best and the brightest.

Since accountants have access to their clients' most sensitive financial secrets, and since they often function as business advisers, they are uniquely positioned to take advantage of their client's trust for their own benefit.

Here's a cautionary tale that was recently reported in *Smart Money*.

A group—hell, a network—of elderly, well-to-do, businessmen hung out together at a country club in Long Island. Not exactly naifs. They socialized at each others' homes; they attended each others' family celebrations; they got jobs for each others' kids; and they invested their money together with the leader of the pack, Sid Schwartz.

To cut to the chase, Sid and his brother Stuart Schwartz allegedly stole $3.6 million from a dozen doctors, dentists, garment-center executives, filmmakers, and even, would you believe, a certified public accountant. (The Schwartzes were not CPAs.)

If it can happen to them, it can happen to you. Checking these guys out wouldn't have helped here. They were pillars of the community.

Here are the warning signs—and they apply to any situation where you are offered an investment:

1. Outstanding, above-market rates of return. The Schwartzes usually promised 14 to 16 percent annual rates of return to their clients.
2. Investment vehicles that are obscure, or that you do not understand, and/or that are not fully disclosed or described to you. The Schwartz deals involved "bridge loans" and "Government of Pakistan (Paki) bonds."
3. A deal that is not open to others but only to "special friends" or the like, and that requires a very speedy decision to take advantage of exceptional circumstances, such as another Schwartz client in distress who supposedly had a desperate need of money and was willing to pay exorbitant rates.
4. Any conflict of interest. The Schwartz pitch always involved an investment where they controlled the books—and the payouts. This also is a flashing red light for all deals where the accountant/investment counselor gets a spiff that is not disclosed or one that is above the going market rate. They don't pay the big bucks for selling sweetheart deals.
5. Get it in writing. Every representation, every promise, every term, every condition. If it isn't in writing, don't do it, no matter how lucrative it may sound and how "iron-clad" the oral representation is.
6. Have your lawyer okay it before you sign it. Make sure to have the lawyer not only go over the terms of the deal itself, but also check out the people involved. Check their:
   - Credit ratings,
   - Judgments,
   - Liens,
   - Criminal records.

   Many a $2,000 suit conceals a two-year stretch in the federal pen for mail fraud. *Caveat emptor.*

Doctors. Lawyers. Accountants. Tough choices, but important ones.

Don't get discouraged.

Make the effort.

None of them will be cheap. So what? A big price may be a small price to pay.

Nor will they necessarily be charming or easy to access, nor even will they necessarily want to do business with you.

So what? This is one time you're hiring sheer professional talent, not customer relations.

If you're the new kid on the block, you should start digging these wells as soon as you hit town. Ask the people in your network who will accept only the best advice, service, and quality in their lives, and find out who they and their peers go to.

M A C K A Y ' S   M A X I M

A bad car deal can cost you a few bucks, but the thing will run just as well as if you got the deal of the century. Bad lawyers and bad accountants can cost you your life savings. A bad doc can cost you your life.

Chapter 17

WHY AIM LOW?

Advice to the new job seeker: Small fish/big pond.

There are several major universities that have well-earned reputations for taking care of their own, but what is less well-known is that there are also companies that have similar reputations both as training grounds and as great places to network—with no onus attached to having only a short tour of duty there at the beginning of your career.

For example, if you're looking to get hired by an advertising agency, the best credential isn't an MBA from a fancy university, it's spending your first two years out of school working for Procter & Gamble, because that's how you learn how it's done.

Hoping to be a marketing whiz? Serving a stint at PepsiCo or one of the company's arms—KFC, Pizza Hut, Taco Bell, Frito-Lay, just to name a few—will impress folks.

In the law biz, it's clerking for an appellate court judge or working in the Manhattan D.A.'s office. In accounting, it's spending time at a Big Six firm, especially going through Arthur Andersen's training program.

In business management, it's a stint at McKinsey & Co., the consulting firm. Not surprisingly, the McKinsey alumni club, which includes Harvey Golub of American Express, Phil Purcell of Dean Witter, Lou Gerstner of IBM, and Tom Peters, is a network made up of business powerhouses who earned their reputations by advising other businesses how to do business.

All these gigs have one thing in common: They represent places where the best and the brightest have started their careers—and lingered just long enough to make peer-group contacts that will last a lifetime. After all, no matter how powerful the rocket, it is only as good as its launching pad.

There is always, always an alumni group.

You may not have graduated from Wharton, played on the Dream Team in Barcelona or Atlanta, or worked for McKinsey. But almost everybody is a member of three or four "alumni clubs" by the time they're thirty.

Remember the civic project you were treasurer for two years ago? That makes you a charter member of the Oak Street Community Center Building Project Alumni Club. How about the summer stock theater group that put on *State Fair* last summer? Or the small band of high-energy executives that helped turn around an ailing software company? Or the group that helped edit a particularly difficult annual report?

They are not always equally useful, but the opportunity for an alumni club always exists in the wake of any exceptional collaborative effort. The Manhattan Project had an alumni club. So do the teams of techies in Silicon Valley who build new computers. So did the participants in Watergate.

MACKAY'S MAXIM
How you start can help determine where you finish. And you can never start too soon. Spend a lot of time thinking about where you (or your kid or your grandkid) should work this summer.

Chapter 18

NETWORKS R US

O kay, you're young. You're on your first job. Your network is a bit thin. You joined the company softball team six months ago, and you're still not a vice president. That's okay. Remember, you learn in your twenties. You earn in your thirties.

When you're starting out to build a network, you should—at a minimum—do the following four things:

1. Hit every trade group meeting you can find: lunches, awards shows, annual dinners, fund-raisers—whatever. It's a prime vantage point for building a résumé and a network. You'll meet the people who work for your competitors—that is, the people most likely to give you your next job. A pretty good bunch to get to know, wouldn't you say?

Also, make an occasional pit stop at the watering hole where folks in your field hang out. These days the watering hole may be a place that actually serves water, like a health food bar, rather than a saloon, but whatever it is, you can be sure a lot of trade gossip is being passed and friendships and amours are being formed. In other words, it's a great place to network.

2. Go to your national trade shows and conventions. It's the way to go coast-to-coast with your network; you will make buddies from

faraway places who could last a lifetime, and if you attend the seminars and workshops, you'll come back with a lot of good ideas.

3. Go back to school. Take classes. Improve your skills. Need a strong recommendation for a new job? Your college prof from five years ago probably can't remember your name. When you're currently enrolled, you have a live faculty contact to applaud your hard work, ambition, and thirst for knowledge. You've upgraded your network.

4. Pick an organization, any organization, and get active. It doesn't have to be the United Way or the heart fund or the cancer fund. You don't have to be Mother Teresa or spend all your spare time reading to the blind. It would be nice if we were all so public spirited, but we're not. So pick something you like, even though it's a bit of a reach to describe it as elevating the human condition.

Join a stamp club. Join a health club. Join a political campaign. Join *something*. Meet people. Build your network.

MACKAY'S MAXIM

Networks may not be for members only, but they are surely for members first.

SHARPEN YOUR EDGE!

Chapter 19

THE SINGLE BEST VANTAGE POINT FROM WHICH TO BUILD

Every organization has certain hot-button positions that put you in touch with all the powers that be within your community. These positions are as powerful as the CEO's job, but they, unlike the chief executives, are available to newcomers.

The message here is clear: Don't ever overlook the possibility of doing well by doing good. Volunteering is the easiest way to add new faces to your network, and it feels great.

Let me tell you about a volunteer position I parlayed into a networking opportunity.

Many years ago I got a call from the chairman of one of our local art institutions. He asked me if I had any interest in serving a three-year term on the board of directors.

He knew I knew zilch about art, and I knew he knew it. My credentials were primarily those of an eager-beaver young business type.

I was flattered. And hesitant. If I accepted, I'd be expected to be an active board member, not a name on the letterhead. It would be tote that barge, lift that bale. No way I could slide.

I asked questions, treading water.

He answered politely. He seemed a little surprised that I hadn't immediately started crawling through the phone to get to the sign-up sheet.

"Can I think it over for a few days?"

He agreed, grudgingly. He was already having second thoughts.

When I called back, I said, "I'd be honored to be on your board, but before I accept, I'd like to ask a few more questions."

"Of course." (Was there a hint of sarcasm in his voice?)

"How many members are on your nominating committee?"

"Let's see. Four, I believe. The chair and three others."

"How often do you meet?"

"Twice a year."

"Look, I know you're not asking me to join because of my knowledge of art or my *Mayflower* ancestors. What I hope you're looking for is to broaden your base of support in the community."

"Actually, yes. It is something like that."

"Well, there's one place and only one place where I can do that. That's the nominating committee."

"I don't quite understand. Why is that?"

"Because the nominating committee controls the lifeblood of the organization. I assume your nominating committee decides the number of board members, the mix, the diversity, who becomes a member, and above all, who the executive committee members, the directors, the officers—like you—will be."

"I see your point, and I see no reason why not."

I accepted. I had asked for enough. But there was a lot more that I left unsaid.

After I joined, we began to meet monthly, not semiannually. At the time there was a constant flow of high-powered executives moving into our state. Like it or not, we were competing with other civic and charitable organizations for their participation. By meeting monthly, when a new honcho at General Mills or 3M or Pillsbury hit town, we were a step ahead of the competition. We were able to snare a lot of the top corporate talent for our board.

I also helped expand the membership of the committee from four to ten members. That too was part of the more-is-better approach. More diversity. More people with a bigger stake in our decisions.

I'm proud to say that these changes played a major role in substantially increasing both our attendance and our endowment.

Then came the happy accident.

I didn't realize it when I joined, but being on the nominating committee was the best single launching pad I've ever encountered for my own network.

Every time a name came before our group for consideration for board membership, or to become an officer or director, we reviewed it.

By the time the ten of us finished the discussion, we knew more about the candidate than about many people I'd known for a lifetime. We knew: interests, background, friends, associates, business reputation, organizations, income, level of giving, capacity for work, hobbies, hot buttons.

More information came out of these sessions than an FBI check for a cabinet post.

And each of the candidates was, by definition, a community leader.

No one had to tell me what to do next. My well was dug. The names—the information—went into my Rolodex. I was ready for them.

When I met them, I knew in advance where our common interests lay, what to talk about, what not to talk about, the building blocks on which to begin a relationship.

All as a result of stumbling onto what appears to be nothing more than an obscure bureaucracy, but is, in fact, the most powerful networking engine I've ever encountered.

Lesson? You don't need a Harvard MBA—sometimes referred to as a yuppie union card—to find a network that gives you access to important people in your community. The nominating committee of almost any civic organization is an open sesame to your community's leadership.

MACKAY'S MAXIM

Find an outfit to join that recognizes you have something to offer, and find out what they can offer you: contacts, exposure, experience. It's all there—in exchange for a little effort.

Chapter 20

MUHAMMAD ALI'S NETWORKING STORY
How I Learned to Expand My Network

Introduction

The world is filled with ex-athletes, ex-movie stars, and ex-pols who had their fifteen minutes of fame and are now forgotten.

Muhammad Ali is one of a handful of exes who not only have retained their celebrity but have grown even more popular over the years.

It was Muhammad Ali who held the torch that lit the Olympic flame in 1996.

It was Muhammad Ali who was seated next to President Clinton and his family on the night of his renomination to the presidency.

And yet it has been over fifteen years since Muhammad stepped into the ring for the last time.

Muhammad Ali may well be the most popular and well-known person in the world.

Today he suffers from Parkinson's, one of the most debilitating of diseases.

Still, he continues to connect with a public that seldom sees him but still adores him. How does he do it?

On December 2, 1975, CBS-TV ran a news story about a social service facility for the elderly handicapped that was about to close for lack of funds. The next day a man showed up with a check for

$50,000 and a pledge of an additional $50,000. He had no obvious connection to the institution, though he was quoted in *The New York Times* (December 3, 1975) as saying "I have a soft spot in my heart for old people, especially the handicapped. One day I might be handicapped."

Ten days later, this Letter to the Editor appeared in the *Times:*

The Senior Citizens Center for the Physically Handicapped at 37 Hillside Avenue in Washington Heights, under the auspices of Self Help (instituted by Jews from Germany), is attended primarily by Jewish people. If it were closed, 54 people would have no other place to go and be left to their solitude. Miraculously and unexpectedly, this center was saved, not by the U.J.A. Federation of Jewish Philanthropies, nor by another Jewish organization or wealthy Jews, but by the heavyweight champion, Muhammad Ali, "The Greatest."

Inside his large, handsome physique beats a big, soft heart that evidently knows no discrimination for charity. Ali did not have to rescue this program for votes or fame, nor does he need to seek Jewish favors. For tax purposes he certainly can find enough charitable causes among his black brethren. Ali may just want to do a good deed. Ali may want to reciprocate the generous contributions to black causes made by Jewish organizations.

Ali demonstrates that minorities should help each other, that we need each other. Ali is a true philanthropist.

Charlotte Wahle
New York

When Muhammad's wife, Lonnie, arranged for me to talk to him, she invited me to their home in Berrien Springs, a tiny country town in Michigan. I flew into South Bend, and booked a limo and driver for the long ride out to his place.

What Lonnie had on the phone called a "hideaway" turned out to be eighty-eight beautifully landscaped acres. The flowers alone could have handled all the weddings in Michigan.

I was met by Howard Bingham, a trusted friend of Muhammad's

for thirty years. He is also a talented photographer who has captured some of Muhammad's greatest moments. Bingham ushered me into the champ's office.

Muhammad rose from behind the desk to shake my hand.

"Hi," he whispered, "I'm Joe Frazier."

That set the stage for six hours of pure, unadulterated fun—and a networking seminar.

Muhammad Ali still has the moves. But now he's a performer and not an athlete.

As an audience of one, I was privileged to be entertained at a magic show, complete with sleight-of-hand, disappearing coins and hankies, and optical illusions.

This was nothing new. Muhammad has been doing these tricks for years. He's quite good at it.

"Watch my feet," he said. He took three steps, turned his back on me, and made himself appear to float three inches off the ground.

Muhammad may no longer float like a butterfly in the ring. Now he does it as a magician.

Once a showman, always a showman. Only the venue has changed.

He still has the 1,000-megawatt smile, the I'm-having-more-fun-than-anyone-in-the-place look, the strikingly handsome features and physique that made him unique among practitioners of his brutal trade.

He has something else too: an essential sweetness to his nature.

The Parkinson's disease that has ravaged his body has neither embittered him nor affected his mind. He spends most of each day answering his voluminous fan mail and signing pictures, books, and boxing gloves for charities around the world to help them raise money. It's not uncommon for these items to be auctioned off for as high as $5,000.

I sat and talked with him while he worked his way through a pile of mail, carefully reading every letter, responding to every request. Three hours whizzed by. Time for lunch.

Add one more permanent lifetime member to Muhammad's worldwide network.

We piled into my limo, but first Muhammad introduced himself to my driver, who told him his name was Francis. Thirty miles later, we rolled into a restaurant. As we were getting out of the car, Muhammad whispered to me, "Tell Francis to join us for lunch."

One thing is for sure: When Francis got up in the morning, picked up his work sheet, and read that he was assigned to pick up an envelope salesman from Minnesota for a routine run, he never imagined that he'd be invited by Muhammad Ali to join him for lunch.

This is what Muhammad Ali keeps busy doing all day long, every day:

- Entertaining his visitors—not with tales from the past but with new talents.
- Rewarding his fans—not with a brushoff, like so many athletes today, but taking genuine pleasure in honoring their requests.
- Showing respect and consideration for everyone—not just the big shots.
- Being generous beyond any expectation of generosity for people of different races and religions than his own.
- Dealing with his own physical limitations in good spirits and with optimism—not with bitterness and self-pity.

Back in 1975, that *New York Times* reporter asked Muhammad why he had contributed to the home for the elderly. Ali responded: "Service to others is the rent I pay for my room here on Earth."

He has paid that rent many times over.

Muhammad Ali is still "The Greatest."

Muhammad Ali's Networking Story

Early in my pro career I was in Las Vegas to fight Duke Sabelong, a big, tall, tough Hawaiian. Gorgeous George, the wrestler, also was in town for a match.

A few days before the fight, Gorgeous George and I were both on the same radio program. They asked me how I thought I would do. I was sure I'd win, and I said so, but it was like "I can beat this guy." That sort of thing. Nothing too flamboyant. Pretty standard stuff.

Then they asked Gorgeous George about his match. He practically tore the microphone out of the announcer's hands.

He called himself the greatest wrestler in the world.

He started shouting about how he was going to tear the other guy limb from limb.

How he was going to kill him, and how he'd cut off his own beautiful blond hair if this guy beat him.

I started thinking to myself, "Man, this is going to be some fight. I sure got to see this fight." And I did. The place was packed. Thousands and thousands of people. Thousands and thousands of people paying to see this wrestling match.

That was not lost on me. Up to then, I had not been exactly shy when talking about myself, but from then on, I talked a lot more. I now understood I would have to do more than just fight. I had to make people want to see me fight. I had to make people care about what was going to happen. Then they'd tell their friends, and their friends would tell other friends, and the excitement would build. These days they call it PR, or spin. I just called it talking. Get enough people talking to each other about you and you've got an audience.

So I learned. I learned how to build a network of promoters, endorsers, and media/entertainment kingpins.

> *Building a network is about paying attention to what people want. I was never a slow learner.*

Let me tell you another story that shows you what I mean.

Just after I turned pro, *Sports Illustrated* did a piece on me, and they sent over a freelance photographer to take pictures.

I got to talking with him and asked him who else he worked for. He said *Life* magazine, which was the biggest magazine in the country in those days.

I sure wanted to be in *Life,* but the photographer told me I didn't have a chance. But I knew if I could make myself stand out, be memorable, I'd make my own chance.

I let it go for a few minutes, and then I asked him what kind of pictures he took. He said all kinds, but his specialty was underwater photography.

So I said to him, "I'm the only fighter in the world who trains underwater. It's like wearing heavy shoes when you do road work so that your feet feel lighter and faster when you put on your other shoes. When you practice punching underwater, with all that resistance, it makes your hands go faster. That's why I'm the fastest heavyweight fighter in the world."

Well, he got real interested, so I said that I'd give *Life* an exclusive if they wanted to do a story about it.

Sure enough, they did. So I got in the pool up to my neck and threw some punches underwater, and he took a lot of pictures.

It was quite an experience, because I couldn't swim a stroke, and I'd never thrown a punch in the water in my life before, but they took it very seriously and did a whole big spread on it in *Life*.

Like I say, I'm not a slow learner, and I pay attention. I listened up, got to know what people wanted, and made my own network.

M A C K A Y ' S   M A X I M

Learn from Ali. Service to others is the rent each of us should pay for our room here on Earth.

Chapter 21

WHEN YOU WORK *ON* YOUR NETWORK, YOUR NETWORK WORKS *FOR* YOU

Network Builder Cards: Part I

(FRONT)

Name _____

Phone (H) _____ (W) _____

Fax/E-mail/Internet _____

Title _____

Company _____

Address _____

_____

Birthdate & Place _____

Connections _____

_____

Family _____

(BACK)

Education _____

Affiliations _____

Special Interests _____

_____

Significant Career History _____

_____

Accomplishments _____

_____

Wow! _____

Unless you have about a gigabyte of available memory in your cranium and can bring up information on demand, you have to write it down. Pale ink is better than the most retentive memory. I've always used a modified version of the Rolodex card to capture the bits and pieces of hot, vital information I collect about the people I meet. These appear as phrases such as "Notre Dame alum," "loves to cook," "never eats lunch," "supports the orchestra," "devoted to kids," "favorite charity is MADD," "divorced twice," and so on.

This all adds up to pounds of papers stuffed in my pockets to be transferred to cards, which I could then use right before my next phone call or meeting. It's a lot of work, but worth every minute, and every top salesperson who gets to me today knows I don't like monogrammed shirts, can't stand waiting, talk to my best friend Lou Holtz every week, and don't eat nuts.

What does that have to do with closing the sale? Just about everything when used at the moment it's needed.

But what about individuals like me who are no longer planted in the office that houses the Rolodex? Because we're in cars, on planes, working from hotels and telecommuting from home, we now need a new set of tools.

The answer, of course, is software. And there are a lot of products out there that can help. *Business Week* recently ran an article describing three different programs: *ACT!, Goldmine,* and *Up-to-Date.* All three can readily organize the basic name, rank, and serial number–type data as well as maintain a history of every fax and phone call you make to members of your network. They can remind you when it's time to touch bases with them again. Properly primed, *Goldmine* can even follow-up on a sales call to a prospect with a letter, a fax, or an E-mail message at staggered intervals. *Up-to-Date* plugs you into the Internet, where you can exchange information and swap lists of contacts.

These programs are out there just waiting to revolutionize your life. But don't let computer illiteracy become an excuse to procrastinate. I've seen Million-Dollar Roundtable members who managed their entire insurance empire from a scribbled-in "little black book."

That's easier said than done, however, when it comes to organizations. For them, networking has always been, and continues to be, a huge information management problem. Sure, your top salesperson or account executive might know the shoe size of every customer who's ever walked in the door. But what about the other people in the office who have to interact with the account? Short of the Vulcan mind-meld featured in *Star Trek,* we have always lacked a way to get information out of one person's brain and conveniently deposited in another's.

The answer, again, is found in bits and bytes, and team selling is getting a whole lot easier. *Sharkware* is a data base software engine that allows companies to connect sales reps or team members in remote locations via laptops with the information they need to do their jobs. It is manufactured by CogniTech Corporation in Atlanta, Georgia, a company I helped found several years ago. (CogniTech can be reached at 1-800-947-5075.)

Whether by hand or by keyboard, the most important priority is to go forward with the concept. And since you didn't buy this book to be told you need to buy something else, let's get going and craft our own program.

Let's start with information you already have.

The first card is you.

Pull out your wallet or purse.

Take out all the business cards you've accumulated. They're not doing you any good in there, so make a nice stack and we'll get back to those later.

Take out all the membership cards. Put those to one side too.

We'll get back to what needs doing as we go along.

Let's start with just names and addresses. As obvious as these are, they can be tricky. You want to be sure both spellings and pronunciations are correct. In the case of tough names, do it both ways: spelling/pronunciation, i.e., Bernstein/Bernsteen.

Also, you should include any preferred nicknames or casual forms of address you may use.

Let's go with the obvious entries first.

The folks. The relatives. *All* the relatives. All your spouse's relatives. If your kids are married, all their in-laws. Pretty soon, it's no longer a family, it's a tribe. Even if you have only ten names on your list, if each one has only ten contacts, you're going to have 100 people in your network.

Now let's compile your personal business list: your barber, accountant, banker, store owners, dry cleaners, insurance agent.

Put a little check mark if you have referred some business to them.

For a mind jogger, go through your personal checks and credit card receipts for the year. Try figuring out how much you spend at each of them and write that number down next to their names. It may surprise you how big the amount is. In some cases, you may be one of their better customers.

Put a check mark against the name if you think you may be a particularly good customer. There's no law against mentioning it the next time you stop by.

"I was just going through my checks, and I realized I spent over $1,500 with you last year. I guess we're really getting to depend on each other more than I knew."

The list is already getting bigger than you thought, isn't it? Along with Mother, you have a mother lode, just waiting to be tapped.

Okay, let's go to the personal list. We're talking friends, neighbors, former classmates, fellow club or church members—all your nonbusiness acquaintances. List the affiliation you have with them; if there's more than one, put a check mark against that name. More than two? Put two check marks.

By this time, I'm sure you can see where this is heading. Not only are you compiling a list, you are segmenting it.

There's the list, and there's the "A" list.

In every major fund-raising campaign, prospects are rated according to their potential. Why? Because fund-raising follows the same 80/20 rule you find in any enterprise: 80 percent of your business comes from the top 20 percent of your customers.

> *If you can identify the top 20 percent of your customers, you always will have a great idea of how to prioritize your time.*

The top prospects are the "A" list.

The more contacts you have with them, the closer you are to them, the greater the volume of business you have with them, the more you have done for them, the more current and active your connection is, the more check marks you will place opposite their names. The more check marks, the more likely they are to belong on your networking "A" list.

In computer networking today, there's a lot of talk about organizing networks around hubs. Human networks have their hubs too—people who seem to be the key "relay stations" for advice or access. Learn who the hubs are on your network and on the networks of your key contacts. They're definitely "A" list material.

It may take awhile to do this, but it isn't that difficult, and if you're conscientious, it will be well worth the effort.

The last group is the meat and potatoes of your business life. Obviously, there's your boss. And then there's your boss's boss.

Do people report to you? Include them.

Now let's get to your peers. They're even more important than your boss.

Why? This cautionary tale will explain: *The New York Times* reported recently that Stephen M. Waters, a managing director of Morgan Stanley, the ultimate white-shoe investment firm, had resigned. Waters had dazzled his superiors during his eight years at the firm, assembling a "glittering list of titles" as he climbed the greasy pole of success.

It seems, however, that his peers had come to regard him in another light.

After heading Morgan Stanley's European investment banking operations, Waters returned to the home office in New York. As he was about to assume his new duties, an article appeared in a trade publication quoting him as saying he "would be taking responsibility for the firm's investment banking relationships." Oh? Wasn't one of his peers handling that assignment?

And hadn't Waters overreached before, when he appeared to denigrate a potential acquisition target in un–Morgan Stanley-like fashion after the deal broke down?

His colleagues wasted no time getting the knives out. One said, "He was ignoring the system and acting very independently." Another added, "Perhaps his view of what his job should be wasn't what the firm thought it should be." Still another really took off: "It was absolutely the death knell for him. People went ballistic. People were out to get him."

Exit Mr. Waters, who probably could recite entire balance sheets from memory but who had failed to assign much value to "goodwill"—the opinion of his peers.

The majority of our network will tend to be our peers, economically, socially, professionally, and personally. Privates hang with privates, not with generals. In Hollywood, a producer wouldn't be seen socially with a lowly writer. Writers go to writers' parties, and so on, up and down the ladder.

> *Your standing among your peers is probably the single most accurate indicator of the value of your network.*

One of my favorite quotes on this subject comes from Conrad Hilton, the hotel mogul. In *Be My Guest,* he wrote "The value of buddies was something you learned in the army, where your life depended on how well a hundred men carried out their assignments."

In the army you were only as good as your buddies.

Once you complete the list of your own organization, add the customers, suppliers, members of professional or trade groups you belong to, and, of course, that stack of business cards we set to one side earlier.

Next group: enemies, competitors, former friends.

The people you need to know the most about are the people who can do you the most damage and who might, if things were different, do you the most good.

Well, things can always be different.

These people can be valuable members of your network. You need a line on them.

Who's going to hire you if you're on the street? Your best shot is with the people who know how good you are because you've been slamming them to the pavement all these years.

I was once in a tough negotiation on an acquisition. We made the deal, even though the lawyer on the other side ran rings around my tiger. The next time around I hired the guy who had handed me my head on the last deal.

And while you are compiling this list, don't forget to include former customers.

Randy was a salesperson for one of the leading radio stations in the city. His top account was an upscale downtown department store, and Randy had a good relationship with the store's advertising manager, Glen. The radio station changed its format to punk rock, and Glen had to tell Randy that none of his customers was into tattoos and orange hair dye jobs, so he wouldn't be able to advertise with him anymore.

Of course, Randy was not too delighted to lose his best account, but he was too smart to burn his bridges. He kept in touch with Glen even though he knew he couldn't sell him anything.

Some of Randy's fellow peddlers thought he was dumb to keep handing out perks to a guy who'd never run another spot unless bankers started showing up for work with nose rings.

Randy had the last laugh. Glen called him one day and told him he'd quit the job with the department store and tomorrow would be named advertising manager of a large brewery. Do rockers drink beer? This Bud's for you, Randy.

Okay, that's it for the names.

We're halfway home. That wasn't so tough.

MACKAY'S (BORROWED) MAXIM

"All my life I have only been as good as my associates, and in them I have found my good luck, my fortune."

—Conrad Hilton

THIS ISN'T THE ARMY
You Need More Than Name, Rank, and Serial Number

Network Builder Cards: Part II

Here is the rest of the information for each of the entries in your network file.

Date

You want to know when you made the entry so you have an idea how old the information is. Each time you update, cross out the old date and put in the new one.

If the update came as a result of a particular occasion, you should jot that down too.

Phone/Fax/E-mail/Internet

Phone alone is no longer enough. I know executives who never answer their own phone but will dash to answer their on-line mail.

Title

Keep this up to date for use in correspondence. Acknowledge promotions and job changes as soon as you hear about them. The pat on the back is back.

Company

Since the first thing that appears on any piece of correspondence is name/title/company name/address, it's also the first thing the addressee notices. I'm always amazed at how much mail I receive that gets it wrong. Being sloppy about these details makes a terrible first impression and greatly diminishes the impact of the message in the letter.

Address

Keep it up to date. When a company changes addresses, sending a short "Congratulations on your new office" note is a great way to stay in touch; it also sends the message that you are well organized.

Birthdate & Place

We make a special effort to make a pit stop on our buyers' birthdays. You wouldn't believe how much business we write up on those days!

I'm a stickler for birthdays, but so are a lot of other people. Therefore, I add the differentiator—birthplace.

For years, I'd had a nodding acquaintance with a very successful person I wanted to get to know better but who seemed totally unapproachable. Then I found out he came from a tiny town of 800 on the Minnesota Iron Range, near the town where my mother was born. Once again, the Iron Range connection proved to be a goldmine.

As was typical of small towns, these two had been great rivals.

The next time I saw him, I said, "I don't care what you think, Cal, but my mother used to tell me that Virginia could beat Orr in any game any day of the week."

I watched the expression on his face change from its normal −40° F state, to bafflement, to a wide grin.

"You devil," he said. "I know about you. You've been reading that damn *Who's Who* again." Totally true. It's a great source for information if the person you're interested in has achieved a certain degree of prominence.

Connections

This is the place to jog your memory as to where you met someone, who introduced you, the names of mutual friends, what activity you shared, and when you last saw one another.

Family

Family names and information about people in your network are important to you because they are important to them. Learn the names, but be very, very careful. I know I have said this before, but I don't think it can be stressed enough. With so many marriages ending in divorce, nothing is more awkward than showing off your presumed knowledge by asking about a spouse by name only to hear that long icy silence that precedes "Muffy and I are no longer married."

It also can be unsettling to find out someone has passed away without your hearing about it, so tread lightly.

Education

Many people feel deeply attached to the schools they attended, particularly college, even decades after graduation. Here's where they began their adult lives and may even have met their spouses. That's why "education," although it is an "affiliation," gets its own line.

Affiliations

This includes memberships in professional organizations, churches, clubs, and political groups. I've met people all over the world and developed some wonderful friendships and contacts based on a mutual membership in an organization. It's a great conversation starter and a reason to stay in touch that can last a lifetime.

Special Interests

Nothing makes a network sparkle more than an exact handle on what makes other people really happy.

You may have already entered it on another line, but do it here too, because this is going to be a line you refer to again and again.

Significant Career History

This includes brief notes on the big moves, up or down the ladder, and names of former employers.

Accomplishments

I really like tracking awards, publications, and achievements, because I know how much effort went into them and how much they mean to the recipient.

Wow!

The stuff nobody else ever thought of, but which, if you can pull it off, is unforgettable.

I have a buddy named Shapiro who walks by the same dry-cleaning place every day on his way to work. Inside the place, visible from the street, is a blackboard, where Terri, the manager, posts various instructions to her employees. One day she wrote, "Check and remove all lint. Remember, it's part of your job."

Shapiro thought this was highly amusing, so when he brought in a couple of shirts one day he teased Terri, saying "Remember, remove all lint. It's part of your job."

The next day when he passed the place, the blackboard had changed. Terri had drawn a big round smiley face and under it she had written "Good morning, Mr. Shapiro."

For days, there was Shapiro's day brightener for all the world to see. He loved it. It put a spring in his step and a smile on his face. Finally Shapiro had a big bouquet of flowers delivered to "Terri—who starts my day with sunshine."

Well, hell, Terri and Shapiro are never going to enter into a big dry-cleaning deal; Shapiro isn't ever going to need to have more than one shirt a day laundered, and before long the flowers will wilt and Terri will have to change the blackboard. So what? They have made the world a slightly happier, warmer, better place for each other than it was before they gave each other a great big Wow! And if that's a network that never yields any other dividend, it's still a great payoff.

MACKAY'S (BORROWED, PART II) MAXIM

"The master in the art of living makes little distinction between his work and his play, his labor and his leisure, his mind and his body, his information and his recreation, his life and his religion. He hardly knows which is which. He simply pursues his vision of excellence at whatever he does, leaving others to decide whether he is working or playing. To him, he's always doing both."

—James Michener

Chapter 23

IF IT DOESN'T WORK FOR YOU, IT DOESN'T WORK

Now you're done with the grunt work. All you need at this point is a system for keeping it in good shape.

Here are some examples:

One young consultant has an ironclad rule that he doesn't leave the office in the evening until he's organized whatever he needs to be entered into the Rolodex the next day.

Another throws everything she collects for the week into a shoe box near the front door and then empties it out first thing Monday morning.

A longtime vendor to Mackay Envelope Corporation has another system. She pulls the cards of all the people she intends to contact during the week and places them in little piles on her desk. One pile is for those she wants to visit personally. Another pile is for those she wants to phone. A third pile goes to her secretary, who prepares envelopes, so that when she has a spare moment during the week she can send a handwritten note.

My own master file has gotten so big that it has become the mother of all Rolodexes and has given birth to a Son of Rolodex that contains just birthdays. That way I can roll through it to an upcoming month and make sure I send a card or make a birthday phone call.

Once a month on a Sunday nestled in my den, I try to review my files. Phone in my lap. Rolodexes by my side, I spin to win. I work that phone so hard it gets as hot as a two-dollar pistol at a Saturday night crap game. I can contact nearly fifty people in one long Sunday session.

TV networks conduct periodic audience surveys to determine who's watching what. About once a year, it's "sweeps" time at the Mackay Rolodex Network. Like the TV ratings, one important purpose of this kind of review is to prune the list to get rid of what's not working. By attrition, by neglect, or maybe by just plain poor judgment, there are going to be a few What-is-this-person-doing-here? cards. Time to pull the plug or write a quickie, How-ya-doing? note and be done with it. Over and out.

That doesn't mean you throw the card away. It just goes in an inactive file. Anything can happen, including your defunct cards un-defuncting.

On the other hand, if you don't want to pull the plug, but you've let the wires fray a bit, then invite your neglected networkee to a let's-catch-up-with-each-other lunch. What's to lose?

You'll also want to identify any gaps in your network. Things change. New situations call for new contacts.

If my business plan calls for selling more envelopes in Madison, Wisconsin, then I better get to know some people in Madison.

Here's another wrinkle: Color-code groups of cards you want to separate by function. Customers are alphabetized behind the red divider. Prospects are alphabetized behind the green. Personal friends and relatives behind the blue, and so on. You can do this with dividers, color cards, or plastic card protectors. Rolodex makes all of them.

Or you can simply code them as you enter them into your computer.

One last suggestion that might prove helpful. Anytime I make a contact, I make a handwritten entry on the card and note the date. This is particularly handy for those quick shuffles through the deck to determine whom I've been in touch with and whom I haven't been.

I've also made a complete copy of my master file, and I keep one at home and one at the office. Now when I add a new card, I make three—one for each master file and one for Son of Rolodex.

Hey, all these mini-ideas are just my way of doing things. You do it your way. The organizing principle here is to make it easy enough so you'll do it and thorough enough so that it works.

All right, we're almost there. We've got the grunt work done. If you let your mind go as you do it, you'd be surprised at all the ideas that will come to you in expanding and cultivating your network. And you'll be shocked by how many people are overdue for a note, a visit, or a phone call.

> *Now that the information is organized either in your computer or on paper, you're in position to use it. It can be your blueprint to success. You can refer to it many times a day. It is a living, breathing document, constantly being added to and updated.*

For example, anytime you recommend one of your network members for something, let that person know. "I don't know if your son has a job yet, Mary, but I mentioned his name to Paul at the bank who had told me he's looking for a young assistant."

Or: "The boss was talking about the new assistant manager job to me, and I mentioned your name. I don't know if you're interested, but when I told him about you, he seemed to think you might make a good candidate."

Win, lose, or draw, who's going to get frosted to hear that?

If you've got something good to say about someone, say it. And make a note of it too.

You don't have to be an anonymous donor. Even though you want to do good, you want to do well too. Networking is networking. Toot your own horn. No one else will if you don't. You've just laid the groundwork for a return favor.

Elmer sold lumber. Elmer's lumber was kiln-dried and cost more to store. As a result, his stuff was always more expensive than anyone else's. Still, Elmer always outsold his competition, because he spent as much time promoting his customers, the builders, as he did promoting his own goods. And they knew it. Elmer was such a factor in their success that when he died, a couple of those builders and an architect who worked for them almost went out of business.

MACKAY'S MAXIM

Keeping a Rolodex is a lot like getting dressed in the morning. It doesn't matter so much *how* you do it, it just matters *that* you do it.

Chapter 24

PLUGGING INTO YOUR NETWORK

Your network isn't the only network you should get to know inside and out. Get to know your boss's core network too.

Everybody has their own kitchen cabinet. When the people the boss listens to become part of your own network, you have that alternate route to get the boss information you think he or she needs to hear.

This approach also works with bosses who listen mostly to themselves. Find out what their interests are, and you not only have an insight into their personalities but a means of networking with them on another level.

These are the right routes to take. Here's a wrong one.

In his book, *Mean Business: How I Save Bad Companies and Make Good Companies Great*, "Chain Saw Al" Dunlap modestly writes, "I'm a superstar in my field, much like Michael Jordan in basketball and Bruce Springsteen in rock 'n roll."

In his third day after taking over troubled Sunbeam, where he very quickly fired half the workforce, Dunlap addressed his front-office troops and suggested that if they wanted to learn more about his management methods, they might buy his book.

One employee asked how much it cost.

I'd say that person (1) should polish up his networking act and (2) is probably no longer with Sunbeam.

MACKAY'S MAXIM

Rule #1: Listen to your boss. Rule #2: Know whom your boss listens to.

Chapter 25

YOU SHOW ME YOURS . . . I'LL SHOW YOU MINE

The most efficient way to expand your network is to trade networks with someone else.

How big is your network? If you answered infinite, you're right. At this writing, you're limited only by the number of people on this planet. And that's if you don't count pets. I know several veterinarians who have made a very good living by being extra nice to the right dogs.

But even if you limit it to humans, your network is potentially the size of all your contacts, plus all your relatives' contacts, your friends' contacts, your business associates' contacts, and so on.

Say you have to send out a mailing to advertise a charity event or introduce a new service you have to offer. Are you going to limit the list to just those names you've been able to scrape together? Of course not. You'll ask me for my list, and if I like the offer I might even ask a few other people for theirs. Instead of a few hundred names, now you have a few thousand.

A word of warning. Remember to treat anyone's contacts with the utmost respect. Like tightrope walking, this is a system based on balance and trust. A fall from grace, like a fall from the high wire, can be very hard to recover from.

When two people exchange dollar bills, each has only one dollar. When two people exchange networks, they each have two networks.

Chapter 26

MAXIMUM EFFORT, MAXIMUM RESULTS

R ay Kroc sold malted milk machines in Southern California in the late 1940s. His best customers were two brothers who ran a drive-in, a relatively new concept at the time. While most drive-ins were tacky affairs, this operation was well lit and clean, with a wholesome family atmosphere, uniform quality at a fair price, and a volume that far outstripped all of Kroc's other customers.

Kroc was a driven man. He knew the brothers were on to something, and he wanted to be part of it. He tried to persuade them to expand so he could increase his own sales to them, but they were content with what they had. Kroc finally persuaded them to sell their concept to him, and he retained their name for his company: McDonald's.

Kroc found a Calvin Coolidge quote that expressed his business philosophy and posted it on the wall of every McDonald's. It reads:

> *"Press on. Nothing in the world can take the place of persistence. Talent will not; nothing is more common than unsuccessful men with talent. Genius will not; unrewarded genius is almost a proverb. Education alone will not; the world is full of educated derelicts. Persistence and determination alone are omnipotent."*

Several years ago, I met Dennis P. Kimbro, a man who makes Ray Kroc look like a hopeless underachiever.

Think of me as the McDonald brothers, struggling along, fairly content with what I had, too busy and not as interested in stretching or expanding my network as I could have been.

Because I'm on the road about 150 days a year, I am not always accessible. You don't have to tell that to Dennis. He experienced it firsthand. Over a period of about three months, Dennis had tried contacting me by phone. He made fifteen calls. He was 0 for 15. He got lots of fancy excuses but no Harvey.

For his sixteenth at bat, Dennis had had enough. He tried a new stance. He called my assistant and threw a "sincere temper tantrum."

"What do I have to do to talk to Mr. Mackay?"

My gatekeeper has been trained to withstand these onslaughts. She does not budge. However, she did explain that I would be on five airplanes in the next five days, "so as you can see, Mr. Kimbro, it will be next to impossible to contact him."

Obviously, "next to impossible" is not "impossible," not to Dennis P. Kimbro, anyway.

"If you will give me the flight number of any one of those flights," said Kimbro, "just the flight number, I don't even have to know the seat assignment. I will be on that flight, sitting next to Mr. Mackay. I will promise you, I will only talk to him for 300 seconds [a tactic he picked up from one of my earlier books]. I will not be a pest. I will not bother him. He will be able to get his work done."

Three days later, on Northwest flight 569, New York to Denver, my mystery date is sitting next to me looking like the cat who swallowed the canary.

He introduced himself, whipped out a legal pad filled with notes, pressed down a button on the timer on his watch, and held it up to me so I could see it. As the seconds began to tick off, he said, "I've got 300—make that 295—seconds to ask for your help, and then I'll leave you alone.

"I've written a book titled *Think and Grow Rich: A Black Choice.* Years ago Napoleon Hill, the author of *Think and Grow Rich,* had begun a manuscript on the question of how Black Americans who are born poor can reach their full potential. Independently of Hill, I had done extensive research on the subject—I have a doctorate from Northwestern—and I was commissioned to update, expand, and finish the manuscript. It reveals how successful Black Americans achieved their dreams and how other Black Americans can apply the same principles in their own lives. For four years, I've been—"

"Excuse me," I said. "You can stop the timer for now. I have to ask you a question. Do the principles include 'persistence and determination'?"

"Why, yes," said Dennis, grinning. I suspect he knew what was coming next.

"Obviously, I haven't read your book, but it's pretty clear to me you know what you're talking about."

Dennis had done his homework. Not only did he know enough to approach me by using one of my own gambits, he also knew that he needed an agent. First-time authors seldom get their manuscripts past editors' slush piles unless they've got an agent. Having an agent put his or her reputation on the line on behalf of an author alerts the publisher that this is a manuscript that deserves their consideration.

"I also would ask you to read it and give me your own views, and if you think it has merit, help me develop a strategy to get some key endorsements and jacket blurbs."

By this time, I knew that if his book was anything like his marketing strategy, it would be a winner. I helped him get an agent—mine, Jonathon Lazear—and some plugs he could use in his marketing, including my own.

Think and Grow Rich: A Black Choice has been a huge success. It has sold 100,000 hardcover copies and gone through ten printings. Dennis has been on the *Today Show,* Larry King, CNN, and CNBC. He's been featured in *Ebony* magazine and interviewed and quoted extensively in many major newspapers.

He is now the director for the Center of Entrepreneurship at Clark Atlanta University, the only program of its type in the nation housed at an historically Black college or university.

As I write this, he's working on his second book, *What Makes the Great Great.*

Dennis P. Kimbro, Ph.D., has made a career as an expert on the habits of highly successful people. He is a living example of his own favorite subject.

I am proud to be part of Dennis Kimbro's network and proud that he is part of mine. I have benefited as much—or more—from our association than he has.

The first person I called when I was in Atlanta for the Olympics was Dennis.

The first person I knew I would write about when I began this book was Dennis P. Kimbro.

There's only one reason that I ever connected with Dennis: his persistence and determination.

You can build your own network exactly the same way.

Do it. Even if it takes more than sixteen phone calls.

MACKAY'S MAXIM
Cream doesn't rise to the top, it works its way up.

EXCAVATE YOUR UNIQUE SKILLS!

Chapter 27

THERE IS NOTHING WORSE THAN LOOKING AT A DEER CAUGHT IN YOUR HEADLIGHTS

Do what you feel comfortable doing, and then do a little bit more, especially when you are first starting to network.

Everyone should learn to stretch beyond their comfort zone.

Don't push yourself to the point where all that people see—and remember—are a cold sweat and a frozen smile.

Force jobs are worse than no contact at all.

I remember once meeting the daughter of the President of the United States at a fund-raiser. I won't tell you which daughter of which president, because I don't want to embarrass her, and let me remind you that Roosevelt, Truman, Kennedy, Johnson, Nixon, Ford, Carter, Reagan, Bush, and Clinton all have at least one daughter, so you can't be sure who she is.

Anyway, I met this young woman for possibly five seconds in a reception line, and the only reason I remember the meeting is that I have never seen anyone so miserable in my life. Even though I had contributed to the election of her dad, I ended up voting against him because anyone who could put his kid through this kind of torture would be willing to put my kid through a lot worse.

This is exactly the kind of impression you are trying *not* to make.

MACKAY'S MAXIM

One reason that people are afraid to network is that they don't want to hear the word no. But no is the second-best answer there is. At least you know where you stand.

Chapter 28

BUTCHER, BAKER, ENVELOPE MAKER

I f you're not a public figure, then there's the inevitable moment when the question comes up: "What do you do?"

I'm in favor of a multiple-choice answer, because it gives the other person a couple of ways to connect. I usually say something like "One, I sell envelopes. Two, I write self-help books. And three, I jog. I'm always looking for ideas for one and two and always trying to figure out how to get paid for number three."

> *Whatever your gig is, put a little pizazz in your answer when asked "What do you do?"*

And prepare it, carefully, even though when you give it, you'll want to toss it off without sounding as if you were reciting name, rank, and serial number.

It's probably the one question you're sure to be asked and, apart from your name, the one thing people will remember about you, so you'll want to use your answer effectively to help build your network.

MACKAY'S MAXIM
There's a reason they call them "connections." You have to connect.

Chapter 29

BE A DIFFERENTIATOR
AND . . .

One of the purposes of networking is to get you to stand out from the pack. If you network successfully, you become known as the person who remembers birthdays, can be counted on to praise a promotion your client just received, and someone who always is just a phone call away.

But what happens when everyone starts to do those things?

You no longer stand out.

This is a problem, especially as more and more people begin to understand the power of networking or, I hope, read this book.

What do you do to make sure you stand out?

You have to use your imagination. And you have to take the extra step.

Let me give you three quick examples.

1. Don't ever send another business Christmas card.

Oh, sure, they are lovely. Sending cards is a nice gesture and everyone does it. But that is exactly the point. Everyone does it. And because they do, nobody remembers them. Want proof?

Ask yourself this: When was the last Christmas card you remember receiving at the office?

> *Don't get lost in the crowd. Instead of sending Christmas cards, send Thanksgiving cards. (There are great ones out there.) Your card will likely be the first holiday impression a person gets.*

Always use a beautiful commemorative stamp. Include a one-paragraph handwritten personal note on the card.

And for the resourceful reader . . . send out birthday cards.

2. Be polite.

You don't think this will make you stand out? You're wrong. We are all too time-stressed. We never can get it all done. These days the person who responds quickly to a phone call or to a note has discovered a true way to be a differentiator.

One of the stories that's told about Billy Graham involves an incident that occurred while he was in a diner with some staff members. When the waitress serving the group recognized Billy, she dropped her tray, scattering dishes all over the place. Graham immediately leaped up and helped her clean up the mess.

How many of us would reach out to another person and help her through an embarrassing moment? Billy Graham's act defined good manners: consideration for the feelings of others.

3. Send a creative present—to their kids.

Be honest, what can you possibly get the Big Kahuna that is actually going to impress her? But if you get her ten-year-old son an autographed baseball from his favorite player or get a well-known person to send a handwritten note to her daughter, you probably won't have a whole lot of problems getting your phone calls returned.

Geraldine Laybourne, a Nickelodeon television executive, found herself seated next to the legendary Hollywood mogul Michael Ovitz during last year's NBA playoffs. Though she had never met Ovitz, she struck up a conversation with his companion, who happened to be his nine-year-old son, Eric.

"Ovitz *père* was impressed," reported *Leadership* magazine. Six months later Ovitz, at the time president of Walt Disney, called Laybourne and persuaded her to leave Nickelodeon to become president of the Disney/ABC Cable Networks. "In her new position, Laybourne will be the most visible woman executive in broadcasting," according to *Leadership*.

She's already proven that she's one of the best networkers in the network business.

MACKAY'S MAXIM

What do you have to offer that makes you memorable? What connects you with the person you most want to be remembered by?

Chapter 30

. . . AND THEY'LL NEVER FORGET YOU

Some things are so basic we overlook them. For example, you don't have a network if they can't remember your name.

Armand Bucci has found a way to deal with that by being the ultimate differentiator.

"Many times I'm introduced to someone new, and they have a difficult time remembering my name. Usually I get Carmen, Herman, or Arnold. I give them my card. On the back it has the different ways to spell my name. They may not remember my name the next time, but they do remember I'm the guy with the card."

When he was job hunting, he enclosed a flyer with his résumé. It went:

If we had to live with 99.9 percent effort we would have:

One hour of unsafe drinking water every month.

Two unsafe plane landings per day at O'Hare.

16,000 pieces of lost mail every hour.

22,000 checks deducted from the wrong bank account every week.

500 incorrect surgical operations every week.

12 babies given to the wrong parents.

20,000 incorrect drug prescriptions each year.

800,000 credit cards with incorrect information . . .

A 100 percent effort makes sense!
Armand Bucci

Armand says that this "helped me get my current position even though my background may not have been as strong as the 150 others who applied for the job."

M A C K A Y ' S   M A X I M

If people keep saying "Tell me your name again," either (a) you mumble or (b) you aren't doing enough to make an impression.

Chapter 31

THE RETURN OF THE ONE-ARMED MAN

Philosophers believe that the Worldwide Web will change the fundamental way we view each other. Networks formed via the Internet will not necessarily be based on race, class, gender, or creed. Disabilities disappear. Opportunities arise in new forms.

Some people think the deck is stacked against them. Mike Brewer can't even shuffle the deck—he has only one good arm. Yet when his handicap threatened to end one career, he managed to use the Internet as his bridge to another.

When we first met Mike Brewer in my last book, *Sharkproof,* he was scratching out a living as a photographer in Hawaii, shooting the showcase homes dotting the Kauai hillside for the real estate industry. The most dramatic and desirable shots—and the toughest and most dangerous to obtain—are overheads. A pilot flies a helicopter over the site and the photographer hangs out of an open doorway and shoots.

Not many two-armed photographers were willing to take those shots.

One-armed Mike Brewer was.

Hanging out of helicopters, legs wrapped around a pole in the open doorway, Brewer shot his pictures with his one good arm.

After Hurricane Eva hit, Brewer went airborne again immediately. This time he photographed the destruction. He got his pictures before the National Guard could clear away the debris and obliterate evidence of the high-water mark—the boundary line for many "pay/no pay" insurance company decisions.

By the time the insurance company claim agents showed up, Brewer was the only person in the world who had exactly what they needed, before-and-after pictures that accurately showed the destruction caused by the hurricane.

Brewer knew what he had—and what it was worth. Over the next few weeks, he made more money than he had made in any single year in his entire life.

Eventually the money ran out, and even his "good" arm, the one that had not been struck by polio originally, began to weaken. He knew he couldn't spend the rest of his life waiting for hurricanes.

Brewer had a satellite downlink TV scanner. Among the hundreds of stations it brought in was the Boise educational TV station, sponsored by a university in Idaho.

Using the Net, he contacted the university and discovered it had gotten a huge grant from the National Science Foundation. The university had used some of it to buy computers, linking up with high schools across the Northwest, using the network to teach physics and simple computer graphics. It was sending photographic images over the network and needed a photographer to help develop the graphics and work the program.

Brewer left Hawaii for Boise and signed on with the TV station. He had to learn computer graphics from the ground up, and he needed to research other programs in other states if he was going to help develop a program for Idaho—and win more grant money.

Instead of hanging out of helicopters, he began hanging out on the Internet.

First major Internet success: access to a U.S. Department of Education downlink for a computer training program for persons with physical disabilities.

Second major Internet success: National Endowment of the Humanities grant to fund "The First Story Tellers." On a tip from a forest-fire crew, Brewer had learned of prehistoric paintings located in caves in the most remote areas of Idaho. The grant would pay for him to fly in, raft in, and film in fifteen of these seldom-seen places. Now he just needed permission.

Third major Internet success: U.S. Forest Service, for permits to film in these deeply hidden locations and create images for their archives.

Brewer's filming has now been completed and tied into other cave paintings found in the West. Soon everyone will be able to see his work on CD ROM or the Internet.

Mike's project, primitive art on the Net, is a unique combination of one foot in the past, one foot in the future.

Though he is slowly losing the use of his remaining arm, Brewer has made the transition from freelance daredevil photographer to computer-based programmer and Internet specialist.

Networking for grants and educational and employment opportunities made it possible for him to continue his remarkable career. Currently he's using the network to search for "hot links" to jobs for graphic art and Web page design. As I write this, he is attending a Federal Webmasters conference in Washington, D.C., on—surprise—still another grant he snared by networking the Net.

Of course, he also has his own Web page. You can E-mail Mike on the Internet at mbrewer @ cyberhighway.net.

MACKAY'S MAXIM
One good head is better than two good arms.

Chapter 32

IT DOESN'T MATTER WHERE YOU START, IT'S WHERE YOU FINISH

My first job, pushing broom in Charlie Ward's "goldmine" was not the fulfillment of my life's ambition. I may not have had much business experience, but somewhere along the line I had bought into the conventional wisdom that there was no such thing as a good job with a broom.

Well, I was wrong. And so is today's version of that homily, for which you can substitute "flipping burgers" for the broom part.

I learned some things behind Charlie's broom that stuck with me. Like showing up on time. Dressing neatly. Showing respect to others. Doing your job. Demonstrating the willingness to do more than was expected of me.

In those days, I wouldn't have known what a network was if I'd tripped over one. But my gut instinct told me that if I could figure out who it was I had to impress with my newly acquired little business-man qualities, I would be able to put the broom down as soon as possible.

Sure enough, within a couple of months, I had been paroled from the plant and was in the sales department. All it took was: (1) being the best broom man of my generation; (2) being sure that the assistant plant manager knew it; and (3) having had the good fortune to have latched on to a guardian angel—someone who was equally eager to escape the goldmine and who took me with him when he wangled his way into sales.

It wasn't until last year, at my own shop, Mackay Envelope Corporation, that I learned that the multiple player deal the assistant plant manager and I had pulled off forty years earlier had a name: "the sausage theory." When one person moves up the chain of command, at least one other moves up too.

In 1993, after a yearlong nationwide search for a president of Mackay Envelope, I had a few candidates who were nines on a ten-point scale but no tens.

We started over. We'd been looking in the wrong nation.

We found our ten, Scott Mitchell, running a division of a Canadian-based company, Moore Business Forms.

When we pitched Scott, he expressed his concern for the people who had moved up the ladder with him at Moore. At the time of his last promotion, when he had moved from vice president of sales to head a division, the vice presidents of marketing, manufacturing, and his second in command had moved up with him.

The sausage theory in action. One link moves. The other links follow.

When Scott came to work at Mackay Envelope, it happened again. His former second in command moved up to Scott's old slot as president. He has now moved—thanks to Scott—to president of one of our largest envelope customers. Good placement, wouldn't you say?

Scott's former subordinates in human resources, marketing, and manufacturing also have moved to more responsible jobs. All of them, incidentally, are Mackay Envelope customers.

Now that's a *wurst* at its best!

Your career can be linked with the careers of others. As your mentors move up, so can you, especially if you have been a key contributor to their promotion or success.

> *It doesn't matter how far down the food chain you are when you start out; networking can pay off big time.*

In some businesses, such as the movie industry, you must pay your dues. They start you off in a major hole and see whether you can work your way out of it. There isn't an executive worth his Humvee who didn't start out in the mail room, the cinematic version of the broom thing. It's like boot camp. Some make it. Some don't.

MACKAY'S MAXIM

There are no dead-end jobs. There are only dead-end people. If you build a network, you will have a bridge to wherever you want to go.

Chapter 33

TAKE MY NETWORK . . .
PLEASE

From the category of life imitates art:

Ten years ago I was in New York to tape a television commercial for my first book.

Unless you count semicelebrity status in Midwest envelope manufacturing circles, I was a total unknown, a first-time author and a first-time TV pitchman.

I showed up half an hour early at the studio.

There, on the set, in living color, was Larry King, holding up his latest book and doing his own commercial. To set the scene properly, it has to be pointed out that playing *The Larry King Show* is to authors as playing the Palace was to jugglers.

He was just finishing up. We were introduced. I went to work. He went to the phone.

Ten minutes later the director patted me on the back, said we're done, and I headed for the elevator.

King was leaving at the same time.

We made a little small talk on the way down. When we reached the door, his stretch limo was waiting curbside.

I started to hail a cab.

He looked a little embarrassed, motioned to me, and said: "Which way are you headed?"

At this point, visions of *The King of Comedy*, a movie that had opened fairly recently, flashed through my head.

In it Robert De Niro plays the wonderfully named Rupert Pupkin, a totally obnoxious and untalented jerk who is obsessed with getting on the talk show hosted by the character played by Jerry Lewis. They first meet when the unsuspecting Lewis offers De Niro a ride in his limo.

"The Park Lane Hotel," I said, Pupkin-like.

"Hop in," said King.

It was only a few blocks. A few blocks to make an impression. A few blocks to be a differentiator. A few blocks to avoid any further traces of Pupkin-ism.

> *If there is any single rule to follow under these circumstances, it's not "How can I get the other person to do something for me?" It's "How can I do something for the other person?"*

I didn't know King's background. I didn't know his likes or his dislikes. I didn't know any organizations he belonged to. I didn't know the names of his kids. I didn't know of a single characteristic, interest, or goal that he and I had in common.

By this time, the limo had already started to pull up to the hotel.

And then a light bulb went off in my head.

Nothing in common—except for one thing. The reason we had gone to the studio.

We both had written books we wanted to sell.

"Mr. King, I hope I'm not overreaching here, but I assume you, like me, showed up at that studio because we'd both like to sell a ton of our books."

"Right on, kid. That's why I write 'em."

King's limo had now pulled up outside the entrance to the hotel, with the motor running.

I may not have known anything about King, but I had done my homework on the publishing business. I began to spill my guts about what I learned. My self-designed, self-taught course had taken me nearly six months. I had talked with over thirty authors, a slew of literary agents, a dozen publishers, a few promotional firms, and six lawyers.

I told Larry King that I had heard the same message over and over: "Many, many good books never see the light of day due to poor promotion, but all the money in the world can't sell a bad book."

"Really?"

"Have you ever heard of Ingram?" I said.

"No."

"Well, not many people have, even though they're the largest book wholesaler in the country. Most people don't even realize that books are wholesaled. They think all a retailer has to do is pick up the phone and call the publisher and order the books. But there's a catch. It takes the publisher three to five days to get the books in the hands of that bookseller—if they haven't run out entirely, in which case they have to go back to press and that can take up to two weeks, or longer.

"If it's a hot book, that's an eternity," I continued. "You wouldn't care to wait three to five days to get a magazine or newspaper you wanted. You'd want it now. Books are like that too. A little like fish. You want 'em fresh or you don't want 'em. Wholesalers have warehouses strategically placed around the country. If a hot book hits and the retailer sells out, they call the wholesaler, and it's instant delivery, sometimes the same day, but never more than twenty-four hours. It so happens that Phil Pfeffer, the president of Ingram, is a good friend of mine. I met him . . ."

"Edgar, turn off the engine, please," said Larry King.

". . . ten years ago at a business conference, and we've stayed in touch ever since. I've visited Ingram. They have more than one hundred talented salespeople stationed by the phones day and night taking orders.

"Now here's the quinella. When a store manager calls from Kokomo, Indiana, and says, 'We're out of Stephen King's new book, please ship us fifty more,' the astute phone seller takes the order and then just might add, 'Say, speaking of King, we've got a new book that just came in. It's Larry King's latest. How about I toss in a dozen of them? I met the author last week. He was here, and he sure is a good storyteller with a terrific message. I bet your customers will like it.' "

King was now on the edge of his seat just staring at me. Even Edgar had turned around to listen.

King did not have to ask me what came next.

"A month ago Phil Pfeffer had me down to his Nashville head-quarters. I gave a pep talk to his sales force and then had a book signing. My publisher had given me one hundred books gratis to pass out to the Ingram sales force.

"If you'd like, I'd be glad to give Phil a call for you if you'd care to make a trip to Nashville. Those people would go crazy to have you call on them. You could give a short speech. Do a book-signing.

"And by the way, did I mention Len Rizzio? He's head of Barnes & Noble/B. Dalton?"

"No, you didn't mention Len Rizzio," King said dryly.

"I didn't know him when I went to see him. His buyers had placed a rather small opening order for my book. I wanted to give him an idea about what I would be doing by way of promoting it, hoping he'd up the ante."

"And?"

"I told him that I'd be going on a thirty-five-city tour—radio, TV, newspapers, the whole bit—and that I'd be happy to *always* mention, on every single show I was on, every newspaper interview I had, that you can buy the book at your favorite bookseller . . . but Len knew I meant B. Dalton. So I said perhaps your people could reevaluate their buy and maybe increase it from 1,500 to 15,000 books, and I'm quite sure you won't be disappointed.

" 'And also, Mr. Rizzio,' I said, 'I have a good memory, and I'll continue to talk up B. Dalton if I ever write another book or two or three.'

"Seven days later, B. Dalton ordered 15,000 hardcover books from my publisher.

"Of course, then I went to Waldenbooks and Crown, to ask why they would be ordering a token amount of books when B. Dalton had ordered 15,000.

"Seven days later Waldenbooks ordered 15,000 and Crown went from zero to 10,000."

King continued to stare. I began to climb out of the limo.

"By the way, do you happen to know Rupert Pupkin?" I asked.

"Pupkin? Sounds familiar. Who's he?"

"Just a guy. Kind of a pest. I think you'd probably want to avoid him."

I don't think it should surprise anyone that I have been on the Larry King Show six times.

We talked about the books I'd written.

We talked about marketing books.

I never mentioned Rupert Pupkin again.

MACKAY'S MAXIM
In networking, you're only as good as what you give away.

Chapter 34

LET THE GAMES BEGIN

Ah, the cocktail party/fund-raiser/charity ball/trapped in an elevator with ten of the strangest people you've ever seen in your life.

Unless you're assigned to the Secret Service detail guarding the president, you're not going to get the guest list for every gathering you attend, so you'll have plenty of opportunities to wing it.

As in most of life's little moments, there's a right way and a wrong way to do it.

Here's the wrong way: "the thirty-second bonding maneuver."

In those thirty seconds, the perpetrator expects you to be convinced that he or she is so very sincerely interested in everything about you. By the way, what did you say your name was?

You can spot these types every time. They're talking to you, but their eyes are trolling the room for their next victim, and on and on and on. The approach is also called "being seen," but this loser doesn't realize how many people are onto it.

Politicians are the worst.

Most have never figured out that it's better to spend time with fewer people at a one-hour cocktail party and have a meaningful dialogue than practice the wandering-eye routine and lose the respect of most of the people they meet.

I learned the right way by observing two of the world's most popular and enduring public figures, Billy Graham and the late Norman Vincent Peale.

When Graham or Peale met someone for the first time, they made that person feel like the most important person in the room.

They made eye contact and kept it.

They smiled.

They listened.

When they talked, they asked questions or made comments that showed they were hearing and were interested in what the other person had to say.

If the conversation was just polite banter, they had a topical joke or a quip—usually a pretty good one.

If it was more substantive, they gave the other person a chance to make a point without interrupting.

When they had to break off a conversation, they did it graciously, by offering to exchange cards and asking the other person to call or write them.

Is it any wonder that these two men created two of the most effective networks on earth?

MACKAY'S MAXIM

Networking is not a numbers game. The idea is not to see how many people you can meet; the idea is to compile a list of people you can count on.

Chapter 35

Q: HOW DO YOU OPEN THE DOOR? A: KNOW THE GATEKEEPER

All peddlers worth their expense accounts try to reach as high as possible on the corporate ladder on the theory—usually correct—that orders from headquarters tend to carry the day. After all, if the folks in purchasing hear "The boss wants you to buy three gross of . . ." you can bet that the purchasing manager is going to do just that.

But those of us who use that tactic also have learned that the higher up we go, the more likely it is that the decision maker we're trying to reach knows exactly what we plan to do. And as a result, that big cigar will have a trusted assistant trained to block our access.

You have to know how to get through.

When I'm selling envelopes, I never place a call to a prospect without first finding out the name of the assistant or secretary. It's easy enough to discover. You simply ask the receptionist who answers the company's main number who runs interference for the boss. Then when my call goes through, the stage is set for a nice one-on-one, because I'm immediately able to address the gatekeeper by name.

Recently I've gotten even better results by not even trying to talk directly with Mr./Ms. Head Honcho.

I tell the assistant, "I would like to work directly with you regarding . . ." an appointment, charitable pledge, study, report, or whatever it happens to be.

> *When I'm talking with the assistant, I'm talking with the person I want to talk to. If the Big Kahuna has enough faith in that person to appoint him or her to that position, that's good enough for me.*

By taking this approach, all I'm asking is that the assistant use his or her judgment to decide if I'm making a reasonable request. If I am, I'm assuming that the assistant is going to give me his best effort to see to it that what I'm asking for gets done.

Over the years, I have had a lot better success working with people in this fashion than in trying to run over them or around them.

Treat the gatekeepers with dignity. Respect their power. And by all means, *acknowledge their help.* Not with lavish gifts. That's gauche. Just little niceties. A creative handwritten note. A humorous card. A plant or flowers. A book. A separate visit where you stop by to see them, not their boss.

Little things don't mean a lot. They mean everything.

MACKAY'S MORAL

Getting through the fence to the top dog is easy, if you know the gatekeeper.

Chapter 36

YOU ARE WHAT YOU READ

You can't make a connection with someone if you have nothing to talk about.

I have one simple tip to make so you are never at a loss: Get yourself a subscription to the Sunday *New York Times*.

> *For a shy person or for someone who worries about running out of things to say, there is no better resource than the Sunday edition of "The Newspaper of Record."*

- It's an encyclopedia of the week's events.
- The movie and book reviews alone are worth the price of the paper.
- If you ever have to talk intelligently about science, travel, sports, politics, or whatever, it's right there.

Oh, yes, the networking part.

They tell me that all the yuppies who summer at Martha's Vineyard line up at the dock every Sunday morning waiting for the ferry to unload its precious cargo of newspapers. You could be in a lot worse company.

MACKAY'S MAXIM

Reading the *Sunday Times* is your ticket of admission to any conversation.

Chapter 37

THE TWO-MINUTE DRILL

I could fill volumes about chance meetings that have changed people's lives, led to jobs, business opportunities, partnerships, new ideas, all just because people sought other people with similar interests.

But the secret is to seek them out.

The two-minute drill can help.

I did this two-minute drill for the first time in my hometown of Minneapolis about a year ago with 1,000 people in the audience. Within two weeks, I'd gotten over thirty-five letters and cards telling me that thanks to the drill, they're now either doing business with the person they met or have a high probability of doing business with them. Thirty-five cards. And I'd bet there were plenty of others who struck oil but didn't bother to write. This exercise is meaningful because almost invariably my mail tells me that it really "jump-starts" the habit of networking.

Here's how the drill works:

I ask the audience members to look around and ask someone they don't know to be their partner. When the whistle blows, they have two minutes to tell that person everything about themselves that they regard as worth telling. A total of two minutes for background, achievement, hopes, dreams, goals, hobbies, marriage, children, frustrations over the Cubs' pennant chances—everything they can think of.

When the two minutes are up, the whistle blows again, and the switch is on. It's amazing what you can learn about another person in just two minutes.

I'll be out of their lives and back home on my deck before the day is over. But the person they just met might be in their lives forever.

> *Never, never pass up an opportunity to meet new people. Your antennae should be up your whole life.*

Remember how you played the dating game? You cruised. You schmoozed. You perused. You worked out. You went to beaches and ballgames and concerts and "singles'" bars. You went to places you'd never be caught dead in today. Why? To meet new people.

Well, why stop now? I'm sure your partner is truly wonderful, but he or she—and his and her many, many equally wonderful friends, associates, and relatives—are not the last people in the world you will ever want to meet.

You know how it's done. You've proved it. You've done it before and you've succeeded. Keep at it. Turn off that tube. Get out among *them.* It can change your life.

Volunteer work. Political clubs. Hobby groups. Service clubs. Church groups. Industry associations. Extension courses. The Internet. The outernet . . . whatever.

And remember this the next time you attend a seminar or speech: The person next to you, or in front of you, or behind you, is much more important than the person at the front of the room.

The point is never, never pass up an opportunity to meet new people. By doing your own "two-minute drill" once a day, you'll meet at least 365 new contacts in just a year's time. Isn't that worth a two-minute investment?

MACKAY'S MAXIM

It all comes down to this:
If you want one year of happiness, grow grain.
If you want 10 years of happiness, grow trees.
If you want 100 years of happiness, grow people.

Chapter 38

THE SHARK THAT GOT AWAY

In football, if you mess up the two-minute drill, there is a very good chance you'll lose the game.

In networking, if you mess up the two-minute drill, there is a very good chance you will miss a major opportunity.

I learned this firsthand on a recent flight.

> *Even though I was flying first class, I figured out a long time ago that both ends of the airplane arrive at the same time. No, it's not because I wanted to impress people. It's because of the people who would impress me.*

I was on my way to do a speech, and I wasn't as prepared as I wanted to be, so I planned on using the time on the plane to make revisions instead of networking.

So, when the woman next to me tried to strike up a conversation, I smiled and told her I was working on deadline. I did the same thing when dinner was served and she offered me her dessert.

Finally, about ten minutes before we were to land, I finished my work. I put away my briefcase and offered my hand to introduce myself and really looked at my seatmate for the first time.

Hmmm. She looks familiar.

Hmmmmmmmmmm. She looks very familiar.

She looks a lot like Diane Sawyer of ABC News.

In fact, she is Diane Sawyer.

I missed my "Prime Time" with Diane Sawyer. It may be a while before I get another chance.

Maybe never.

MACKAY'S MAXIM

Networking is like sports. Even a small infraction can cost you the game.

DIG DEEPER!

Chapter 39

A LEAGUE OF HER OWN

This is one of the best stories about persistence, resourcefulness, and creativity that you'll ever read.

For several decades, until she passed away in 1995, Erma Bombeck was one of the most successful, widely read, and beloved syndicated columnists in America.

She tapped a vein in the American experience that no one else even knew was there.

Erma wrote about the average American housewife, the unglamorous, unappreciated, unnoticed American mom who spent her life schlepping kids and pets and groceries, took out the garbage, fixed the meals, cleaned the house, worried about her weight, occasionally trailed toilet paper from the heel of her shoe, all the while trying to maintain some modicum of feminine allure.

When Erma first had the urge to write about these experiences, she knew she had a problem. It wasn't that she didn't know the territory. For thirty years she had been a housewife raising three kids in Dayton, Ohio. Her problem was convincing the overwhelmingly male power structure that ran the newspapers that what she had to say might be of interest to their readers.

Or, to be more specific, she knew the guys who ran the *Dayton Journal Herald* didn't have a clue.

Why should their readers find anything interesting or humorous about the life of an average housewife who complained about things?

Bombeck knew she would somehow have to engage these editors through their networks if she was going to succeed. But how?

Bombeck knew the all-male editorial group was unlikely to ever become her biggest fans. But their wives were. The question was how to get to their wives.

She researched where the paper's editors lived. It was in a suburban community with a small weekly paper, the kind that's always eager for "filler." She talked that small weekly into running her column. It was not the editors of the *Herald*, but their wives, who saw her work, fell in love with Erma, and persuaded their high-powered husbands to run her column in their paper.

Within two years, Erma Bombeck was in syndication across the county.

"She made her own luck."

So wrote her longtime friend, Ann Stephenson, who told how Bombeck got started in an article in *The Arizona Republic*. She made it because she did her homework and used what she had learned to reach the people she needed to make part of her network in order to succeed.

> *The only people who are lucky building their networks are the ones who work day and night making their networks succeed.*

It would have been easy for her to stay in her assigned slot, the acknowledged wit of the weekly bridge game, never known beyond her immediate circle.

She didn't. She busted out. And even though it took her years to become an overnight success, she did it and connected with an entire generation of American women who saw her both as a role model and as someone who truly understood and could express the meaning of their own lives.

Erma Bombeck understood that if she could ever get published—even in a weekly shopper—women would identify with her and want to connect with her. Identification? Connection? Hey, that's what a network is all about.

Bombeck used her network creatively, to tap into another network that was beyond her reach.

It was a brilliant strategy—and it worked.

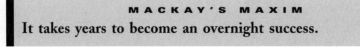

MACKAY'S MAXIM

It takes years to become an overnight success.

Chapter 40

BRING SOMETHING TO THE PARTY

When my supervisor at Quality Park Envelope dragged me along into the sales department, he knew I wasn't just deadwood pushing a broom. I'd done everything in my power to convince him I was a player. A player without many plays, sure, but he needed me.

Likewise, when Scott Mitchell's people moved up and out, they weren't just tagging along. They'd paid their dues and proved their value long before the move ever happened.

Notre Dame football coach Lou Holtz wanted to play football when he was in high school. There was just one problem: He weighed only 130 pounds and wore Coke-bottle glasses.

Holtz didn't get much playing time. He was a fourth-string guard. The coach put him in the game only when the other three guards went down or the game was hopelessly out of reach. So Holtz learned all the other positions. He was still a fourth stringer at every one of them, yet: (1) by giving the coach something he could use, Holtz increased his value elevenfold; and (2) Holtz had also increased his own chance to get what he wanted elevenfold.

Most people think they can get by on charm alone. I wouldn't advise it.

Another fellow I'll call "Wade" is an assistant football coach at a Midwest state university, which has a Division One football program. Wade can barely tell an "X" from an "O." He's there because of his ability to recruit high school players in the Chicago area.

Chicago is a treasure trove of athletic talent, and numerous Wade wannabes are constantly combing the rosters for prospects. Almost every major football program has a recruiter responsible for Chicago. They all have networks and the competition is brutal. More turf battles have been fought there than in Bosnia.

Wade flies in about twenty times a year to meet with the most important members of his network, the Chicago area high school football coaches. He counts on them to let him know which players are legitimate Division One prospects. If his relationship is solid with the coach, he can expect help in recruiting the player.

So far, Wade's recruiting technique is identical to what the other recruiters do. They all keep in contact with the high school coaches and the school principals in their area, looking for standout ballplayers.

What does Wade do that the others don't?

He goes a step further.

Wade's secret is how he handles his other network: the parents.

Often the outstanding high school athlete is the first person in the family ever to have gone to college or even to have been away from home for any length of time.

Wade becomes the parents' eyes and ears while their son is away at school. He lets them know how the young man is progressing academically, athletically, and personally. And if there's a problem, Wade lets them know that too. As a result, when Wade finds himself competing with another recruiter, he has an ace in the hole: the parents of his previous recruits.

He asks them to call his new prospect's parents. They usually are glad to do Wade a favor. Sometimes the two sets of parents even know each other.

"Wade calls us every week," they'll tell the anxious parents. "He calls us more often than our own son does."

It may not be as effective as it was having Lou Holtz in your living room, holding a Notre Dame jersey across your son's shoulders and telling you he was born to wear it. But if you didn't have Holtz, and Wade doesn't, it sure can help.

Wade has job security because of his ability to provide a network that others find extremely valuable. If something goes wrong with this job, he'll be snapped up in a minute by another school.

> **MACKAY'S MAXIM**
> It's great to be liked. You'll have a network you can always use. Once. It's even greater to be needed. You'll have a network you can always use. Period.

Chapter 41

DIVERSIFY

Don't build a network that looks just like you.

The power is in diversity, so diversify—starting with age. When you're just starting out, the older members of your network are likely to be in much better position to give you a leg up than your peers.

When you get to be a geezer, you need the younger members to give you a sense of what's "in" and what's "out." You're sure not going to get it from the Guy Lombardo ("Who's he?" you ask) crowd.

The same goes for the benefits you'll receive by adding different gender/religion/education/race/income level interests to your network.

You're not going to have much of a reach if your networks consist of nothing but clones.

MACKAY'S MAXIM

If everyone in your network is the same as you, it isn't a network, it's an anthill.

Chapter 42

LOVE, HONOR, AND OBEY YOUR SPOUSE'S NETWORK

My best friend is my wife, Carol Ann.

I'm not going to get gushy about it. Discussing, exchanging, loving, caring, and understanding are not the same as agreeing.

We have profoundly different ways of doing things.

I'll give you an example.

There we sat in a crowded stadium watching a heated match at the U.S. Open Tennis Tournament.

Twenty thousand spectators were in the stands concentrating on the game. Carol Ann had other priorities. She was carrying on an animated conversation with the woman seated next to her.

I aimed a few pointed glances at my bride. No effect whatsoever. Then a loud "shhhhh." Totally ignored. By then I was so distracted I missed the winning point. To make matters worse, Carol Ann didn't.

"That was not only the deciding point, that was the best-played point of the match," she declared. Then she went back to her new-found friend.

Since I seemed to lack the ability to follow the bouncing ball, I eavesdropped on my wife's conversation. Carol Ann was explaining that while we were in New York City, we had visited our daughter, Mimi, who had recently earned an advertising degree and moved there to crack the job market.

What a coincidence! The mystery lady told Carol Ann that she happened to work for an advertising agency. She gave Carol Ann all sorts of tips about which firms were good places to work and which were sweatshops, who was hiring, who wasn't, who really called the shots on the hires, what they were looking for in their applicants—in other words, pure 24-karat gold, the sort of inside information that a job seeker would kill for.

Did Mimi, this daughter of a tennis-loving family, like to play tennis?

Did Bugsy Seigel like to shoot craps? Mimi was captain of her college tennis team.

Bottom line: Not long afterward, Mimi was hired by the same agency.

Hey, it can happen. That's why you keep networking, particularly if you can do two things at one time, which Carol Ann can do and I can't.

> *If I were to generalize a bit, I would say that there are observable differences between the way men and women network.*

Men's networking is less "friendship based" and more business oriented. We choose our social partners as much for business reasons as we do for personal reasons, and we have few reservations about inflicting them on our spouses.

Women tend to be less overt in constructing their networks, and they are inclined to rely more on personal compatibility rather than cold-blooded, neutral facts.

When a working wife wants to entertain another working woman, she'll tend to take her to lunch, sans spouses. The working man's style would be to make it a foursome for dinner with all spouses on board.

Men tend to use sports as a networking tool. Women don't.

Women are more apt to share personal information, particularly about their spouses. Men don't.

When married women with children network, they talk about their children. At length. When married men with children network, they talk about their children rarely if at all.

Women can be more subtle, more observant, and often more effective than men in their networking. What man could tell you what the couple they had to dinner the previous night were wearing, and what it said about them? What woman couldn't?

Note the differences. Don't confuse them with weaknesses.

The point is, there's no such thing as a "best" style. Networking is a lifetime learning process. If you have a spouse or partner with a different style from yours, good for you. Open up your eyes and ears; you're bound to learn something.

MACKAY'S MAXIM

Vive la différence. **Benefit from it.**

Chapter 43

THE BEST PLACE TO FIND A HELPING HAND IS AT THE END OF YOUR ARM

The two most significant developments in networking over the past few years have been the emergence of the Internet as a networking tool and the growth of nontraditional networks, particularly those for the benefit of minorities and women.

> *The new networks are part of the ongoing democratization of our national power structure. The old boys' network is still firmly in control, but more and more people who don't conform to the prototype are grabbing for the steering wheel by developing networks of their own.*

The New York Times recently ran a story about Black business networking. They include the National Black MBA Association, the National Minority Supplier Development Council, the National Association of Black Women Entrepreneurs and the National Association of Black Architects. There are now 150 of these groups, nearly double the number in 1981.

"Because the system is not user friendly," says Jacqueline Dickens, who runs a consulting firm with her husband, "African Americans and other people of color cannot afford to wait until someone adopts them. They must do something active and proactive. They must cause upper-level white male managers, who have connections with people in high places, to mentor and sponsor them."

One wise mentor took a young African American vice president at J.P. Morgan under his wing and wanted to help him learn the cultural rituals of the White power structure. He urged him to take up golf. The article doesn't tell us whether he also advised him to follow the ancient prescript: Never beat the boss.

Affinity groups exist for every racial, religious, gender, educational, and occupational preference. If you're, say, a Hispanic female civil engineer with a degree from Purdue, I count "Hispanic," "female," "civil engineer," and "Purdue" as four ready-made networks.

Of course, there is no reason to limit yourself. If you also like jazz, write poetry, garden, and jog, you've got four more that are based strictly on interest rather than background.

MACKAY'S MAXIM

Of course networking is work. But nobody ever said it can't be fun too.

Chapter 44

THE NETWORK RIGHT IN YOUR OWN BACKYARD

Neighbors make up one affinity group that is too often over-looked in this drive-through day and age. You know, those people who live up and down the same street you do.

Neighbors are part of your network. And, unless you're the Unabomber, you're going to have a certain amount of contact with them, like it or not.

And a certain number of shared concerns.

Schools

Streets

Noise

Taxes

Crime

Zoning

Pets

And so on.

Most of the problems that arise from these subjects will come as a big fat surprise to the new homeowner.

Although it only makes common sense to do your due diligence before you make one of the most important purchases of your life, I'd hate to estimate the percentage of people who leap before they look and buy a new house.

"Oh, the real estate agent didn't tell you about the new halfway house for derelicts on mind-bending drugs that's going in next door to you?"

How odd.

Don't wait for the housewarming party to meet your new neighbors. Start your network before you sign the purchase agreement.

Over a period of thirty-five years, Carol Ann and I have bought or rented a half dozen homes. Each time, before we bought, we would go door to door knocking together.

After all the usual pleasantries, or—even more revealing—unpleasantries, we'd ask the questions. I'm sure you know them.

"How are the schools?"

"Are there enough kids of the same ages as our kids to play with?"

"Any crime problems?"

"What are the people in the neighborhood like?"

"Anything going on that might affect the neighborhood, like a zoning change?"

And the clincher: "What would make you want to move from this neighborhood?"

I can think of a lot of homes we did not buy because of the hidden liabilities that those questions uncovered: a railroad that was blocks away yet still a noise problem at 4 A.M.; an elementary school that was in turmoil over the curriculum; and a violent and quarrelsome couple whose domestic brawls often spilled out onto their front lawn.

You are not going to catch those nasty divots in the Happy Hollow landscape when you're cruising through on a Sunday afternoon.

A little legwork can save you a lot of heartache.

There's another benefit. Wherever it is you do finally decide to buy your home, you've jump-started your neighborhood network.

You don't have to knock on the door *after* your purchase and introduce yourself. Been there. Done that.

There is, however, one sure way to destroy your neighborhood network (and possibly your neighborhood) overnight.

The night your kid graduates from high school and you decide to host a party. After the psychiatric examination, if you are certified as sufficiently sane to resume functioning in society, there are two things you must do.

Must do.

MUST DO.

Hire security. (This is where you call your cop network friend and hire a couple off-duty cops.)

And for God's sake, be sure to invite all your neighbors. As long as they're going to be up all night anyway, they might as well have a front-row seat. Noise from the band. Noise from the kids. Congestion. Cars parked on lawns. Unseemly activity and inappropriate behavior. Other things, terrible things, things you never dreamed possible at Happy Hollow.

Don't worry, they'll get you back. Just as soon as their kids graduate.

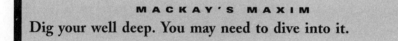

M A C K A Y ' S   M A X I M

Dig your well deep. You may need to dive into it.

Chapter 45

COME ON IN, NO SHARK SIGHTINGS TODAY!

It's relatively easy to develop an open give-and-take with friends; it's harder with acquaintances. But what about customers? They're part of your network too, and they deserve to be heard—and listened to.

Several years ago I was the keynote speaker at a meeting arranged by Corning, the glassware people, for their top 500 customers. Corning is a $4.8 billion company with a proud history. More tourists visit the Corning Glass Museum each year than go to Niagara Falls, 140 miles up the road.

Fifteen minutes before I was to go on, the national sales manager took the stage.

He asked the audience to reach under their seats, where they would find a hand-held remote control device. The lights dimmed, a screen lowered behind him, and a series of multiple-choice questions appeared.

The questions were designed to determine what Corning's customers thought of the company and its products.

The customers were asked about price, service, quality, performance, variety, features—virtually everything that could have an impact on their buying decisions.

"You will have total anonymity and confidentiality," said the sales manager. "This is not a love-in. We want your honest opinion."

The questions rolled by. It was push-a-button, give-a-grade, rating from 1 to 10, as I recall.

Now comes the amazing part.

When the questions had been completed, Corning displayed the results for the audience.

It wasn't pretty. Some of the responses had to have been embarrassing to the company. Many others were very positive. But it took a lot of guts for Corning to hang their dirty linen out to dry in front of their customers—their best customers.

No matter. The sales manager was effusive in his thanks.

"You have given us exactly what we asked for and exactly what we needed," he said. "Honesty. We intend to deal with you in the same way. With honesty. To try to correct those things that concern you. To never stop attempting to improve. To do everything within our power to win your approval and your business. We can't survive without you, and the only way we can survive with you is to meet your needs.

"We thank you for your perception, your insights, your willingness to tell it to us like it is. We hear you. Now I would like to present our featured speaker . . ."

Well, believe me, that was the toughest act I've ever had to follow. I've been a peddler since the snake sold Eve the apple, but that was the first time I saw customers who were ready to climb over their chairs to place their orders.

What's networking? Most of the time it's pretty pedestrian—I'll help you/you help me. However, on too many occasions it doesn't reach the level of an honest exchange. And isn't honesty what we all need the most?

MACKAY'S MAXIM

The riches of the world pale in comparison to the value of an honest opinion.

Chapter 46

MARILYN NELSON'S NETWORKING STORY
How We Got the Super Bowl

Introduction

What hasn't Marilyn Nelson done?

She currently serves on a dozen volunteer boards. That's just currently, because there have been many more over the years. Marilyn also serves on the boards of such household names as Exxon, First Bank System, and U.S. West.

Her lengthy list of awards is studded with such tributes as "caring" and "service" and "leadership" and "community." She's even received the equivalent of a knighthood from the king of Sweden and a similar award from the president of Finland. She has no equal as a truly generous, devoted, untiring volunteer. She's also warm and witty and always great to be around.

Marilyn is vice chair of the privately held Carlson Companies, a $12 billion enterprise headquartered in Minneapolis. Her father, Curt Carlson, recently announced that he intends to turn over the reins to Marilyn. Yes, it's the same Curt Carlson who is Minnesota's most famous billionaire businessman. But listen up. Curt is not the type who would turn over a hot dog stand, much less a multibillion-dollar business, to his offspring if she couldn't cut it.

She can, and she's proved it many times over.

Here's what she told me.

Marilyn Nelson's Networking Story

As Harvey has pointed out, I'm just a girl who can't say no. I like being a volunteer, and I like being with other volunteers. Volunteers are charged with energy, their projects do a lot of good in the community and can be fun too.

I came to know Minnesota Governor Rudy Perpich when I chaired Scandinavia Today on behalf of the National Endowment of the Arts and Humanities. Since one thing usually leads to another, particularly when you have a reputation for doing volunteer work, I must have made it onto the governor's Rolodex.

He asked me to chair Minnesota's Super Bowl bid. What I know about football can be put into a very small, very unsuper bowl, but I do know something about promotions and enthusiasm and just plain old putting on the glitz.

It takes a network, a really, really big network.

Like the governor's, my Rolodex is no slouch either.

There are 5,000 names on it representing every cross section of the community, from police to bureaucrats to dance bands to window painters, bakers, bankers, even ice castle builders.

We needed all of them for this party.

How do you get 100,000 visitors to Minnesota in January?

Why, you call it the Great Minnesota Warm-up.

And you enlist an army-size network of talented, supercharged volunteers to keep that thermometer perking.

The volunteers moved smoothly from their previous roles parading with Scandinavian flags to parading with Super Bowl T-shirts, from singing Scandinavian national anthems to singing football fight songs.

Well, we got the Super Bowl—there was no blizzard that day either—thanks in no small part to the heartfelt prayers of millions of Minnesotans—and many people who go to every one of these events said it was the best-organized Super Bowl they had ever attended.

Our network is so strong I believe we could organize a global event within days if necessary.

Anyone in need of a 10,000-voice choir, just let us know.
Let the games begin! (Just practicing.)

What Marilyn left out was a key part of the story because she is so humble.

> *It is all very well and good to put an infrastructure in place to handle the Super Bowl. It is quite another to convince the owners that they want to come to Minnesota in January to watch the game.*

Most people would have begun by lobbying the commissioner of the National Football League, Paul Tagliabue, to get him to award Minnesota the site. But as Marilyn intuitively understood, that wasn't the way things are done in the NFL.

The key man to see first was the then-owner of the Philadelphia Eagles, Norman Braman, who was head of the Super Bowl site selection committee.

Marilyn dispatched me to see him, and then, at her direction, the committee took the extra step. We went and lobbied each of the twenty-seven other owners individually.

When it came time for them to vote, it was all over but the shouting. Minnesota would be hosting its first Super Bowl.

MACKAY'S MAXIM
You can't get anything done—no matter how good your network—unless you understand the process.

Chapter 47

DON'T FORGET THE ONES
YOU'VE LEFT BEHIND

Don't forget—or underestimate—the power of people who have recently left the company or organization you have in common.

> *Just because they've moved on is no reason to yank their cards. In fact, there's a reasonably good chance they'll become even **more** valuable members of your network.*

Whatever new connections they make may well be connections you currently don't have.

There's another situation you might want to think about too. That's when a couple you've been close to gets divorced.

Not infrequently, both former partners disappear socially off the radar screen so far as their old network is concerned. Often it's awkward for them to try to keep up these friendships as individuals with half the team gone.

In my opinion, the intact couple should at least make separate social overtures to each member of the divorced couple. Don't abandon your friends just because their situation changes, even when it changes for the worse. Life goes on. They'll need you, probably more than ever.

MACKAY'S MAXIM

Out of sight doesn't have to mean out of mind. People drop out of sight for reasons, usually the wrong reasons—job loss, illness, divorce. Don't let them get too far away.

Chapter 48

TEACH YOUR SUBORDINATES THE POWER OF NETWORKING

Tim was a young life insurance salesman. He came from a blue-collar background, and his primary network consisted of the bachelor beer-drinking buddies on his softball team. Of his three best friends, one worked at the Ford assembly plant, one at a service station, and the other was between jobs.

Tim's boss, Walter, was a great insurance salesman with good contacts in the monied community. Walter had grown up in a country-club environment and graduated from an Ivy League school. His classmates and friends were upper-middle-class professionals whose lives were as remote from Tim's world as the other side of the moon.

When Walter developed a training program for Tim, he neglected to allow for the difference in their backgrounds. Walter couldn't understand why Tim couldn't sell the big policies.

It was no surprise that Tim didn't make it in insurance. He didn't have a network, and he wasn't properly coached on how to develop one or in how to deal with people who came from different backgrounds.

Tim was bright and personable. He just wasn't handled right.

His next job was with a utility company. The utility put Tim through an intensive two-month training course that grounded him in the fundamentals of the business but, most important, furnished him with information about the prospects and customers. It didn't matter

who Tim's friends were. It mattered how well he could develop relationships once he had a solid start. He became very successful.

Could Tim have made it in life insurance? Sure.

Many successful insurance salespeople didn't go to Harvard or belong to the Social Register. Tim just needed someone other than a
stuffed shirt like Walter to show him the ropes.

A second example will hammer home the point.

Jack was another blue-collar type. In the home where he had grown
up, the drinking glasses had begun life as jam jars. Jack was trying to
work his way through college with a minimum wage–type job, and he
just wasn't making it. In desperation, he decided to take on a second
job.

He answered an ad in the college newspaper for direct sales work
selling aluminum cookware. The market was young working women
away from home for the first time.

The entire sales force consisted of young, good-looking, male college students.

Jack quickly learned that there was more to selling pots and pans to
single women than being able to explain the relationship between the
gauge of aluminum and the conductivity of heat.

In this situation, the chemistry between salesman and prospect was
a lot more important than the metallurgy. Jack was a hard worker, an
eager learner, and he had good people skills.

He was trained in prospecting as the key to building a successful
sales career. It was hammered into him that whether you made the
sale or not, each sales call must produce three more leads.

Jack was so good at it he was able to quit his other job, and he
made enough money to get him through college.

He even married a woman he met when he was peddling his pots
and pans, "even though she never even bought a potholder from me."

After college, Jack decided to make selling a full-time career. His
boss was Milt, who, like Walter, was a great insurance salesman. But
unlike Walter, Milt knew that most insurance salespeople fail not
because they don't know how to sell but because they don't know how
to prospect.

For months Milt took Jack with him to meetings, to clubs, and to every other place there were people who could buy his product. Since Milt was old enough to be Jack's father, he reasoned that some of his friends' children would be prospects for Jack.

It took a while, but Jack steadily developed a network. Milt had taught him how to move in circles that could afford to buy from him, but Jack made his own luck.

Milt has since died, but in the last fifteen years or so of his life, he was semiretired and he worked for Jack. The agency is Jack's now, and he has a sizable sales force working for him.

Are you a manager? If you are, you know that your results depend largely on the contributions of your subordinates. They'll do a much better job if they're good networkers. Don't forget to tell them they'll also be helping their own careers too.

MACKAY'S MAXIM

Teaching subordinates to network is one of the best invest-ments in the future you'll ever make. And by the way: Is your boss doing the same for you?

MACKAY'S ''TWO-FOR-ONE-SPECIAL''
MAXIM:

You can build a network with any set of tools, so long as you know how to use them. Any competent carpenter can build a house, but no two carpenters have the same tool kit.

Chapter 49

NETWORKS FOR SALE

You need high-level advice and you don't yet have the high-level contacts who can give it. Solution? Hire the network you need.

I had to do that when I first went into business for myself.

By that time, I was pretty knowledgeable about sales and marketing. I'd spent five years selling envelopes, and I could do it in my sleep. But who wants to spend the major portion of their waking hours sleepwalking?

I wanted to run my own show instead of working for someone else. I scraped together every dime I had and went into hock for what seemed like the rest of my life to buy a nearly bankrupt envelope manufacturing company and a few broken-down machines that went with it.

If you're in manufacturing, there are two concepts that you have to master: (1) making your goods at the lowest possible price without sacrificing quality and (2) selling those goods at a higher price than it costs you to make them.

Simple, right? Then why, after three years, did I find myself teetering on the edge of Chapter 11? I was doing all right on number 1, but number 2 had me on the ropes. In those three years, I had gone through three factory managers, and I still couldn't knock out an envelope and sell it at a profit.

So I decided to try to find a consultant who could help me. My reasoning was this: There were 200 competing envelope companies in the country. None of them was about to give me a plant tour. I had no formal engineering background. I had no network of spies to tell me what the other guys were doing right that I was doing wrong.

The right cost-specialist consulting firm probably had been in at least twenty-five of my competitors' plants. I could either put on a fright wig and a putty nose and try to talk my way into them as an OSHA inspector, or I could buy that knowledge.

Machine speeds, output per hour, rejection rates, productive capacity, waste—what does a guy like me know about this stuff? It would have taken me half a lifetime to comprehend what I needed to meet my own needs.

I had to have an expert. So I bought one.

I asked everyone in my then-meager network to suggest a consulting firm, and the name that kept popping up was Spencer Tucker and Associates.

Thirty years later, my Spencer Tucker and Associates cost system still lives at Mackay Envelope. The system has been profitable every year since it was installed.

This consulting firm has now worked with more than seventy-five envelope manufacturers and eventually became, in my opinion, the #1 adviser to my industry.

My own network couldn't provide me with the technical answers I needed, but it did help me connect with an outfit that had the network that could.

They were worth every penny.

Good advice is never cheap. Cheap advice is never good.

Maybe you need help to find a new job, locate a house, advise you on investments, improve your professional skills. It's certainly nice when you can turn to your network and get it for free. But sometimes you can't. Better to hire the best advice you can at any stage in your career. Too often you'll get what you pay for.

MACKAY'S MAXIM

You can't always be an expert. You can't always know an expert. But you can always hire an expert.

DON'T FALL IN!

Chapter 50

HARVEY'S TOP-TEN LIST
of the Biggest Networking Mistakes

Take it from an old grizzly who's been there and done that. We like to think that with age comes vast experience. Guess where that vast experience came from? That's right. Until someone invents a Teflon-coated suit, the most penetrating insights come from hindsight.

Is there a bright side? Sure. The more you learn from everyone else's mistakes, the fewer you have to make yourself.

Here are a few goodies:

1. Don't assume the credentials are the power.

As every salesperson knows, the key to the sale is knowing who's got the hammer.

If it isn't the purchasing manager, it's the person who writes up the specs.

If it isn't the person who writes up the specs, it's the person who draws up the budget.

If it isn't the person who draws up the budget, it's the person who's the boss of the person who draws up the budget.

If it isn't the person who . . .

You get the idea.

Every outfit is different. No organizational chart can tell you who the real decision maker is.

There are a lot fewer powerless titles these days than there used to be. The downsizing tide has swept away the corporate empty suits and birds in gilded cages.

The people who are left are exercising greater power than ever before, though often their titles don't reflect it. The most important decision maker often can be found lurking behind the most inconsequential or incongruent title.

You need a network to find out where the power is.

2. Don't confuse visibility with credibility.

Al became active in his church. Soon the church directory mutated into Al's networking file. If there were two people standing around the vestibule, no matter what they were talking about, Al would try to turn the conversation to investments. It got so that some of the members hated to have him around.

One congregant said, "I'm a welder, and I sure don't come to church to talk about welding."

Church committees that were always looking for a warm body gave Al the cold shoulder.

To no one's surprise, before long Al drifted away from the congregation and joined another to try his luck there.

Moral?

> *Don't join any organization, particularly a religious organization, solely to advance your own interests. Your motives will be as painfully obvious as a deathbed conversion.*

3. Don't be a schnorrer.

That's Yiddish for people who constantly take a little bit more than they're entitled to. (That's as opposed to a *goniff*, who is an outright thief, and a *nudge,* who is merely annoying. Yiddish provides endless gradations for defining difficult people.)

Save your big-favor requests for the big issues. Keep a running balance in your mind of what you have asked for and what you've delivered, and don't overdraw your account.

4. Don't say no for the other guy.

Okay, you do need a big favor.

Don't presume that someone within reach of your network would automatically say no. If they're able to do it, and it's worth asking for, then don't be afraid: Ask. Am I contradicting what I wrote a moment ago?

Hopefully, no.

Use common sense. It's one thing to make a pest of yourself or to overreach. It's quite another to be afraid to reach out for help when you really need it.

I suppose if I were asked whether it's better to err on the side of caution or incaution, I'd say, if the stakes are high, I'd risk the "begging" factor and go for it.

The worst they can say is still no, but at least you didn't say it for them.

5. Dance with the one that brung you.

Learning to network is no more an option for life insurance salespeople than learning to march is an option for army recruits.

It's basic training.

Life insurance salespeople are taught to network from the get-go and are expected to continue to network throughout their careers.

Each company has its own terminology for describing and organizing its networks. At Steve's company, the list was segmented into such categories as Centers of Influence and Recommenders. Steve was a successful life insurance agent.

As a local salesperson, Steve was always asking his favorite Recommender, Howie, for leads. In the early years, every time Howie recommended a prospect to Steve, he'd hear back immediately on how it went. If Steve closed a sale, he would send Howie a nice thank-you note and take Howie and his wife to dinner or drop by Howie's office with a bottle.

As time went by, Steve tended to get lax with his role in the equation, and after a while, Howie quit referring.

Howie is semiretired now, his kids have all left home, and he's a bit out of the loop.

Steve may figure Howie won't be buying more insurance or have the contacts to provide insurance leads, and he's probably right.

But insurance agents don't just sell insurance anymore. Howie told me he just bought a mutual fund. He didn't buy it from Steve. He bought it from the agent who sells insurance to his kids.

When someone in your network comes through, don't be a stiff. Dinner, flowers, a box of candy, a bottle of Old Faithful, a card, or even a phone call is called for. Remember, these people didn't have to extend themselves for you. But they did.

And here's a tip: Be sure to thank the person at the top. No one ever does, because they think he or she hears all day long what a super job their company is doing. A heartfelt "thank you" will be music to their ears. Do it and you'll be remembered.

6. Don't mistake the company's network for your network.

Corporations need networks to do their jobs efficiently, keep their customers, and save the company.

A major reason for downsizing isn't just foreign competition. It's that management has discovered the value of networking. By concentrating on improving networks between employees, companies can eliminate bottlenecks, bring products to customers faster, pare expenses, and increase profits.

Management has learned that the traditional hierarchical organization pyramid slows them down. The fewer the number of people who have to sign off, the more quickly decisions can be reached, the more quickly the product cycle can be run, the more customers you keep, and the better the chances of the company to survive. Good-bye to five layers of decision making and paperwork and hello to the people who can get the job done.

Better networking = fewer people.

If you're going to keep your job, your network has to be as good as or better than your own company's.

You need:

- Support and sponsorship in other departments besides your own, so that you're able to jump to another department if yours is downsized or jettisoned.
- Lines of communication that tell you what's happening in other parts of the company—who's growing, who's shrinking.
- An outsider's objective view of your company and how industry-wide trends are affecting your role in it.
- Foreknowledge of what skills are going to be in demand at your company.
- A backup strategy in case you are let go—in other words, a career network outside the company.

Think your company is going to provide you with this stuff? No way. There's just you and your own network.

7. Don't be slow to answer the call.

There's a call on your answering machine. You know that it's a request for help and that it's going to take some time and trouble on your part to respond satisfactorily.

Do you stall? Do you ignore it?

Don't.

Even if you never expect to have your effort repaid. Remember that your network will be as fast broadcasting your failures as it is in broadcasting your successes. Maybe no good deed goes unpunished, but no bad one goes unreported.

8. It probably isn't just your network that's aging; it's you.

Phone not ringing quite as much as it used to?

Maybe that's because not as many people are using the phone.

They're using E-mail, faxes and the Internet.

If you're an old fud like me, you probably have an old-fud network.

Well, old fuds retire, or get sick, or become obsolete a lot more than non-fuds do.

As a result, unless you make a genuine effort to modernize your skills and knowledge, your network is shrinking. Your network value is being limited by your underdeveloped skills and knowledge.

A little earlier I wrote about Howie and how he started doing business with another insurance agent because Steve, his old agent, hadn't bothered to stay in touch and even failed to extend even a few elementary courtesies to his old client.

Well, even if Steve had been casting bouquets at Howie's feet, Howie still might have dumped him.

Why? Because Steve had gone stale.

Mutual funds? Why bother? Steve made a good living selling insurance. He knew it backward and forward. He didn't need new ideas or new products. Most of his clients were happy with what he had to offer.

But times change. Howie had money to invest. He wanted to see it grow. He knew there were tremendous investment opportunities among companies that were developing new products or were taking advantage of the technological revolution. He needed someone in his network who could help him find them.

Howie wasn't about to entrust his hard-earned savings to a guy who didn't know E-mail from V-mail.

Your network is only as good as the knowledge and information you can bring to it.

If they are old and stale, what kind of network do you think you're going to have?

Catch the *Zeitgeist*. (This one ain't Yiddish. It's German. It means "spirit of the times.")

9. Don't underestimate the value of the personal touch.

The big supermarket chains sell their bread and other staples as loss leaders. Wal-Mart advertises and sells power tools at a lower price than small store owners can buy them.

If you're running a small business and you're competing with giants, how do you manage to survive?

It's critical for small businesses to be able to network. "High touch" is your equivalent of a loss leader. It's what gets your customers in the door and what keeps them there.

If your customers think you are better than the competition, you probably are. The key is to find out what makes them think so and then exploit it to the max.

How do you do that? Ask: Why do your regular retail customers buy from you and what do you have to do to keep them?

Let's say you own a bakery. Did you grow up with your customers and go to school with them?

Do you attend the same church? Live in the same neighborhood? Belong to the same clubs? Do business with each other?

If you don't meet any of the specs listed above, have you hired any people who do? Have you hired their kids to work in your shop?

Do you sponsor a team? Contribute your goods for fund-raisers? Advertise in the community and school papers? If you run a small business, there are countless ways of becoming better known.

Do you have a signature product or service that can be promoted? Fresher goods? A few seats where customers can enjoy coffee with their rolls? A free tray of samples on the counter? A cinnamon roll twice the size of any other?

Do you get all the gettable wholesale business in the area? How many restaurants or company cafeterias are there that you can make part of your network? How many of them could you get if you designed a delivery schedule to fit their needs? The big supermarket may not be as accommodating or reliable as you. Would it pay you to expand your territory a few miles to pick up some new accounts?

The hardware store, the independent meat market, the service station, and all the other neighborhood businesses have to go through the same exercise.

> *Small businesses that survive and prosper know how to network with their customers and prospects by emphasizing a level of personal service and attention that the big businesses can't.*

There's another benefit to that approach. If you know who your customers are, then you'll also know when some of them stop coming by with the same regularity. Mail a card. Tell them you've missed them. Offer them a free loaf of your new raisin bread just for stopping in and saying hello again. It's worth some expense to keep an old customer because it costs so much more to get a new one.

10. If you don't know, ask. Even if you do know, ask.

Many small business owners do not want to show their naïveté and are afraid to ask questions. Yet the big guys are constantly trying to stay abreast of customer concerns with focus groups and sophisticated monitoring techniques. To compete, draft a questionnaire and put it where customers can pick it up. This method is inexpensive and could provide you with valuable feedback.

And if you want to quadruple your response rate, throw in a P.S. that every week there will be a drawing for two football, basketball, baseball tickets . . . whatever.

A final thought. Suppliers are also a great source of information. You are their customer, so they have a vested interest in your success. You'd be surprised at the wealth of information they have if you just tap it. "There's a bakery about your size in Happyville, and they put in a little coffee bar. He tells me it brings in over a hundred bucks a day with hardly any expense." "The hardware store over in Sunnydale started specializing in underground watering systems and added a new skate-sharpening machine, and they're really going gangbusters with it."

A small business can develop a network of epic proportions. The small businessperson can be more creative than a national chain and can tailor-make promotions to their target audience.

MACKAY'S MAXIM
The wise person isn't the one who makes the fewest mistakes. It's the one who learns the most from them.

Chapter 51

NORMAN ORNSTEIN'S NETWORKING STORY

What Not to Do to Win Friends and Influence People

Introduction

The *Columbia Journalism Review* has called Norman Ornstein "the nation's hottest pundit." The *National Journal* refers to him as an "icon of the press."

Norman is a resident scholar at the American Enterprise Institute for Public Policy Research. He serves as an election analyst for CBS News and for fifteen years was a contributor and consultant to the *MacNeil/Lehrer News Hour*. His latest book is *Lessons and Legacies: Farewell Addresses From the Senate*. Others include *Debt and Taxes; The People, Press and Politics;* and *Vital Statistics on Congress,* now in its eighth edition.

Norm and I met through the Young Presidents Organization, and we've shared the platform together at several international meetings.

He's a gifted writer, teacher, and storyteller. See if you don't agree. Here are two great networking stories about avoiding mistakes.

Norman Ornstein's Networking Stories

In the 1970s I found myself spending a huge amount of time on the phone with reporters. I still do. It has meant that I get quoted a lot in newspapers and magazines and sound-bitten on television. That in turn has earned me the moniker "King of Quotes," which has stuck with me since.

One reason reporters called me was that I returned my phone calls as promptly as I could. When I was a young professor starting out, I would call major political and journalistic figures from time to time to ask a question. Some would return my calls, some would wait until a second call or a third from me to call back—and some would never call back. That hurt. Sure I was a no-name pisher, but it was common courtesy to call someone back. And I determined that I would not be that way if I ever reached a stature where people would be calling me.

But I also came to realize why it was difficult sometimes to return all one's calls. Sometimes I would have deadlines; sometimes I would have a huge stack of messages. It was tempting to prioritize the calls, not by when they came in but by stature—return the calls from *The New York Times* and the *Washington Post*, not the ones from the *Omaha World-Herald* or the *Fresno Bee*. There was a surface practical reason to do so. Getting my name in the *Post* or the *Times* would mean that powerful people would see me quoted, and would add to my respect level, while nobody I knew or cared to know would read the Omaha or Fresno papers.

Remembering my own years as a pisher, I tried not to operate that way. And after a while, I saw graphic reasons why I was doing good and doing well at the same time. It turned out that there are people I knew and cared about who do read the Omaha, Fresno, and the hundreds of equivalent papers out there—the politicians who live in their cities or represent them and their states. And it turns out that they care far more about what is written about them in their local papers, even the tiny-circulation weeklies, than in what the *Times*, *Post*, or *Wall Street Journal* have to say.

If I was quoted saying something about George Mitchell's actions as Senate Majority Leader in the *Washington Post*, I rarely heard anything about it. But any comment or observation I made that was in the Portland, Maine, paper got an immediate response from Mitchell—positive or negative. The same has been true for literally dozens of other major political figures from Kansas to California, from Michigan to Montana. What started out as something done for good manners turned out to be something of considerable benefit—and I learned that talking to, and being respectful to, people who seemed to have little apparent stature can have big payoffs.

Here is a related story.

During the Reagan administration, a delegation of network executives went to see President Reagan about the syndication issue (a bitter conflict, with huge economic stakes, between television networks and Hollywood producers over who would retain syndication rights for television series).

They had to cool their heels for a long time in an anteroom, where a young man was seated at a desk to keep them company while they waited. They ignored him—after all, a junior staffer among network presidents was not to be treated equally, or recognized at all—and conversed about their strategy, as if he were invisible.

The young man turned out to be Craig Fuller, a young but powerful White House staffer who had as much role in decisions like the syndication one as anyone else in the White House. In one stroke, they ticked off Fuller, turning a potential friend and ally into a skeptic, spilled some of their lobbying strategy to a key player, and alienated a young man whose power and role grew by leaps and bounds as the Reagan presidency went on.

MACKAY'S MAXIM

Never assume that a junior person is a meaningless person; he or she may be or may end up being more important than the big name. Treating everybody with dignity and courtesy is not only good manners, it is good policy.

Chapter 52

DON'T MAKE A MOVE WITHOUT IT

Once you've spent all this time building and documenting your network, you sure don't want to lose it if you change jobs. It would be hard to think of a bigger mistake.

We're all concerned about whether we can keep our pension and medical benefits in place if we switch employers. How about your network? To be *permanent*, it must be portable.

But is it truly?

Let's say you're a salesperson. Does your company view your Rolodex as company property?

I doubt if many of us know the answer to that. I wouldn't suggest asking your boss.

My guess is: Some companies do and some don't.

Don't wait to find out until it's too late.

If there's a dispute on this issue, you're going to be in much better shape to protect your interests if you have a copy in your possession.

Make one. Keep it at home. Maybe the office copy is theirs. Who knows?

But the one at home? If you made the copy on your dime, on your time, and keep it in your home, why, that's yours, isn't it?

MACKAY'S MAXIM

In a world where information, jobs, and even whole companies are transient, only your network is permanent. Safeguard it.

Chapter 53

SPIN TO WIN

O ther people's opinions of you have an enormous impact on your life. What's the buzz on you? Good? Bad? Everyone needs a cheering section—and let's face it, everyone needs a means to combat the negative stuff.

An important new player has emerged on the political scene in recent years: the spin doctor.

The spin doctor's role is to develop, advocate, and broadcast a positive response to every situation that affects their tiger.

The good ones are at their best when their boss looks the worst.

Bill Clinton's spin doctor's finest hour was her skill in dealing with the "bimbo eruptions" that kept popping up during Clinton's first presidential campaign.

Bob Dole's spin doctor managed to sell the line that his less-than-impressive response to Clinton's State of the Union Address was a targeted appeal to a narrow constituency of delegates in the Maine caucuses, who craved red-meat right-wing rhetoric.

Any of it true?

Members of the press are often too lazy or too busy to investigate the charges and too cynical to believe the answers. They just print them both—and leave it for us, the public, to reach our own conclusions.

This is networking at its most primal level: fighting fire with fire. Your enemies' network vs. your own network.

If this all sounds too silly and melodramatic, think for a moment. Have situations arisen in your life when you've been hurt by ugly rumors?

Have you simply stood by and let it take you down?

You don't have to be helpless when this happens. Get your own spin doctors to get your word out, or you risk looking desperate.

- It's not true.
- It's old news.
- The source has an ulterior motive.
- The situation has been exaggerated and misunderstood; here are the facts.

If it's an attack that's likely to do lasting damage, don't keep taking hits without fighting back. Counterattack through your network.

Drawing on these resources is a lot more effective than staying mum and trying to wait it out.

It shows that you have allies willing to stand up for you.

It gives your loyal friends the opportunity to defend you.

It will teach your enemies that you will take no unanswered blows.

Start spinning.

MACKAY'S MAXIM

Your network is the best, most emphatic, and most credible reflection of your success and your talents.

Chapter 54

NETWORK ALERT

Now let's look at "spin" from a more positive perspective.

When your name is in play for a major promotion, a new job, a big business deal, you should prepare your network to go proactive.

Judges are awesome at this. Learned. Solemn. Powerful. Black robes. Sitting on a dais. Sworn to be "fair and impartial."

And there go the judicial candidates, scrambling around, calling in favors from their networks to write letters and pass resolutions on their behalf.

Candidates for judge flood governors and senators and presidents with recommendations from peers and pols.

Why? Because it works.

If it doesn't bother judicial candidates to use their networks to lobby for them, why aren't you doing it?

Who's supporting you? Just you?

What does that say about your leadership talents?

Your organizing ability?

Your standing with your peers?

Your friends?

The strength of your network could very well be a key ingredient in whether or not you get what you're after.

Alert the active portion—your former bosses, colleagues, instructors, bankers, neighbors (yes, neighbors)—that you may need them.

Are they on board for you? Don't take them for granted.

When was the last time you touched bases with the people listed as references on your résumé? You don't want to find out that the members of your cheering section: (a) aren't your ardent supporters anymore, (b) can no longer be found at the address or phone number you've listed, or (c) are no longer living.

Hmmm.

"Guess we won't be talking with Rollo's old college dean. He expired five years ago. Maybe Rollo knew that and didn't want us to contact him. And if Rollo didn't know it and still has him listed, what does that say about Rollo?"

Stay in touch. Turn your network proactive.

Birds do it, bees do it, even judicial nominees do it.

MACKAY'S MAXIM
R.I.P.-Rolodex in Pursuit. Let your network lead the charge.

Chapter 55

NETWORK INTELLIGENCE

Another distinction we all need to make is between information and gossip.

If you're on the receiving end, you may have to wade through a lot of the latter to get much of the former, but that's the price you pay. It takes a ton of dirt to yield an ounce of gold.

It's when you're on the delivery end that you can have real problems. Once you develop a reputation as a gossip, you'll never shake it, and whatever useful and truthful information you have will be mightily discounted.

It's like your virginity. Once you lose it, you can never get it back.

MACKAY'S ''BORROWED'' MAXIM
"Two great talkers will not travel far together."
—George Borrow

Chapter 56

NETWORKING POSTER CHILD

A network can pin you up. But it can also pin you down.
One person who is living testimony to the power of networking is Bob Packwood. But his pin-up shot looks more like a wanted poster.

It wasn't until women began networking with each other that they began to realize that Packwood was a serial sexual harasser who had been at it for years.

Packwood's case was one of many that came to light when women began to caucus with their networks to exchange information and confirm their experiences regarding the creeps who were doing this stuff.

The increase in the number of reported harassment cases is not necessarily the result of more harassment. It's the result of more networking.

MACKAY'S MAXIM
Just because you're not networking doesn't mean nobody's talking about you.

Chapter 57

ALL NETWORKS ARE NOT CREATED EQUAL

Too many people fail to distinguish between social acquaintances and their true, influential network.

I know I have.

I remember waltzing into a buyer's office, certain I had a gimme, and being told, "Just because I knew you when we were kids doesn't mean I'm going to do business with you now."

Substitute "played golf," "drank beer," or "hung around together" for "when we were kids," and there isn't a salesperson alive who hasn't been blown off in this same fashion.

Yesterday's network is not today's network.

Your social network is not your business network.

Your "money" network is not your "experience" network.

Don't assume that one network automatically flows into another. Sure, you want to make the stretch. Any good sales rep would love to convert every relative he can trace back to Adam into a customer, and tries to. But it isn't an automatic. You have to lay the groundwork, the same as in any other business situation, and not presume that anyone *owes* you the honor of doing business with you.

In this country, doing business is a privilege, not a blood debt, although a social or a family relationship certainly can ease the way.

A lot of doors have been slammed in a lot of faces, including my own, of people who assumed they had a network that didn't exist.

MACKAY'S MAXIM

Don't fish for trout in a goldmine or pan for gold in a trout stream.

Chapter 58

ASK AND YOU SHALL RECEIVE—MAYBE

L et's say you're in the fund-raising business.

You make an appointment to see a prospective giver.

You ask for $5,000.

The cold, hard fact is: He only has a capacity to give $500.

You have embarrassed him by asking for too much.

The $500 he was willing to give would now make him feel like a piker.

The result?

You get nothing.

Had you done your homework, checked with your network, you could have scored a nice contribution.

Cost of lesson: $500 and one live prospect.

MACKAY'S MAXIM

When you're asking for what you want, take into account what the other person can give. Overplay your hand and you're likely to come up empty-handed.

MINDING THE WELL!

Chapter 59

HARVEY'S TOP-TEN LIST
of the Best Ways to Stay in Touch with Your Network

1. Use the calendar creatively.

Sure, send birthday and anniversary cards, but recognize your networks' other special days. If you have an Irish client, call or drop a card or take him or her to lunch on St. Patrick's Day. If you have someone in the Far East in your network, call before the Chinese New Year.

Then there are the Jewish holidays, like Hannukah and the Jewish New Year. You don't have to be Jewish to send a card, and believe me, it will help you stand out from the pack.

There's also Kwanzaa, which is becoming increasingly popular among African Americans as an addition to Christmas.

(I'll know some of this stuff is working when an African American friend tells me he sends out Hannukah cards and gets back Kwanzaa cards.)

As always, though, be creative.

No one who received a Christmas card from the comedian Red Buttons ever forgot it. Buttons's personal notes were uncannily on-point, precise references to his most recent contact with the recipient. The note would read something like "I'll never forget meeting you on April 15 (or whenever it was) and getting the dish on this year's Yankee pitching staff (or whatever it was)."

How could he remember the date and the conversation so accurately eight months after it occurred?

Well, he couldn't.

As soon as he met someone, no matter when it was, he made out their card, included his personal note, and stashed it away until the holidays. To the best of my knowledge, he used the same system for years, and no one ever caught on.

Never underestimate the power of a simple thank-you note, remembering a date or a place that's important to a member of your network, or a note of congratulations.

Yes, Mom was right. Little things mean everything.

2. Watch for important community events.

Here's another place where you can use your awareness of your network's group affiliations to connect.

Let's say your network includes this year's chair of the local Red Cross drive. Attend the annual meeting, or send in your donation—without being asked—in his or her name.

By the way, whenever you donate to an organization or a political campaign, there's an old bit of street wisdom that goes: The more hands it passes through, the more people who know about it.

3. Observe organizational/personal/company changes.

Local papers and magazines all have business columns that feature significant new hires and promotions. When one of your network members lands on the list, you can be sure every stockbroker in town will send a card, so hand-write yours or make a phone call. Or you might try something a little more creative, like a personalized pocket pad with the person's name and new title on it. I wouldn't send an office plaque unless you're sure it conforms to the corporate culture. They're very visible and may be too showy.

I've got a little edge here because I'm in the envelope business. I send some attractive personal—not business—stationery. It shows I care—and it shows my product.

4. Get wired.

E-mail and Internet addresses are becoming as much a part of doing business as telephones. When a network member creates an electronic address, send an E-mail to establish that you're part of each other's electronic network. (By the way, be sure to put your Internet address on your business cards.)

5. Clip and ship.

You can stay in touch with your network just by reading the paper. All you have to do is be sufficiently aware of your members' interests occasionally to clip an article or a quote that might interest them.

I've been a runner for thirty years, and the running network is one of those self-absorbed little subcultures in which people are constantly passing on tips to each other that can help them become better runners, or at least improve their tolerance for the physical and mental stresses of running.

I do a national weekly newspaper column, so when I wrote the following I clipped it out and sent it out to my running buddies:

> There are only two times in your life when you want to get older. When you're 15, and the minimum age for a driver's license is 16. And when you're 59 and a competitive runner, and next year you get ranked against 60–64-year-olds instead of 55–59-year-olds.

6. Use your pit stops constructively.

There are active members of your network who you won't see from one year to the next. Never neglect them when you're in their area, even if it's just a layover at the airport and you can't visit with them personally or take them to dinner. Be considerate. Call.

Next time you go out of town, and you've checked with your network to find out "What's a good place to eat?" bring back menus and send them to the people you asked. I always include a note: "Great suggestion. The food was terrific . . ." and when I can get away with it: "and the bartender says he remembers you well."

Remember to bring back copies of the local paper to the members of your network with connections to the town you're visiting.

Once I got a note back a couple of weeks later:

Dear Harvey:

Thanks for mailing me that copy of the *Winston Salem Journal.* You'd have no way of knowing this, but there was an obituary in it that really floored me. My best buddy in high school passed away. I hadn't seen him for years, and it might have been more years before I found out about it. At least I was able to send Gwen (his wife) a note. I don't have the foggiest recollection of ever having told you that was where I was from, but I'm sure glad you remembered.

7. When your network is filled with static, you can help clear the air.

Is one member of your network at odds with another? You can be an honest broker and help them resolve their dispute.

I won't kid you, this is a high-risk proposition. It's quite possible that one—or both—of them will wind up blaming you.

Every family has members, even entire branches, who aren't speaking to each other. Whoever named the TV show *Family Feud* didn't have to explain the title. Fortunately, most families also have a go-between who manages to handle the necessary communication between the warring factions.

If you've got the personality to do it, go for it.

A network should not be viewed just as a tool for your own personal benefit. Used properly, it can work for the benefit of others, and that applies here.

Just remember, everyone loves to boo the umpire.

8. Anyone can call them when they're up. Remember to call them when they're down.

One of your network members has lost her job. Now is the time to offer her any help you can in making a new connection.

Sending flowers to someone in the hospital is appropriate. Sending a hot meal to a coworker or an employee who has just had a family member come home from the hospital is an especially thoughtful, and an especially rare, show of consideration.

Two minutes a day reading the obits will tell you more of what you need to know than a lifetime poring over the box scores.

My mother died in 1955, when I was twenty-two. After the service, sitting in the car reserved for the family, I watched the people walking down the steps as they left the synagogue. It was a big funeral. There were a lot of people. At that moment, with my mind's eye, I took a group photo. To this day, every person, every face is firmly fixed in my memory.

When you need help, it surely lightens the burden to know you have a network of people that you have helped. Once you get into the habit of helping others, it's satisfying in itself without regard to any possible reward.

9. Report any major changes in your situation.

You've been promoted. You've changed companies.

You've just joined the Little League, or the Junior League, or the American League. Tell your old network about your new network. It gives you an opportunity to stay in touch. It gives them an opportunity to expand their networks.

10. Be there.

Sure, you can skip the wedding and send a spoon, but don't. Weddings, confirmations, graduations, school plays, bar mitzvahs, recitals, the big award: People always remember who was there and who wasn't.

At our shop, we make a big deal out of birthdays. We even close the switchboard for ten minutes or so and catch the calls on an answering service so that no one is disturbed when we present the honoree with a cake and recognize the special day.

I've sweated harder over composing my remarks for one of these events than I have for a speech to an audience of CEOs. When I'm in town I would never dream of missing one.

Most businesses hold an employee appreciation event at least once a year. And then there's the annual Christmas party, picnic outing, whatever . . .

Bosses who duck out of these are making a big mistake. If you want a network with your fellow employees instead of a nice big pyramid with you in your assigned spot on the top, I'd suggest you make it a point to be there.

MACKAY'S MAXIM

Two things people never forget: Those who were caring to them when they were at a low point, and those who weren't. Elevators go *up* and *down*.

Chapter 60

IT IS BETTER TO GIVE
BEFORE YOU RECEIVE

Network members who call you when they have something that might be an opportunity for you, rather than when they need something from you, are "A" listers by definition.

By the same token, you'll make a lot more "A" lists yourself by being proactive on behalf of your network rather than reactive.

> *If you could have a bird's-eye view of a networking transaction, it would resemble two people working a cross-cut saw. Round 1: One side pushes. The other side pulls. Round 2: The pusher pulls and the puller pushes.*

Lyndon Johnson had his own unique strategy for playing that game. Johnson liked pushing better than pulling.

He was said to have kept two jars on his desk: "Favors Due" and "Favors Owed." He saw to it that the "Favors Due" jar was always twice as full.

Put your memory where your mouth is. If you want to impress people with how much you care, show them how much you remember by doing favors for them before asking them to do favors for you.

MACKAY'S MAXIM

The old 80/20 rule still holds true. Twenty percent of your network probably provides 80 percent of the value. What have you done for them lately?

Chapter 61

THE EVER-BLOOMING GARDEN

Woody Allen said that 80 percent of life is just showing up. Don't neglect the other 20 percent.

That's when you want the other folks to show up.

Every understudy and second-string quarterback knows he may be only a sprained ankle away from stardom.

You can and should plan ways that recognize the value of your network.

1. Events

I have always been partial to events that bring your network to your own doorstep in a social setting.

The Billy Graham Evangelistic Association has an annual luncheon for its suppliers. It's a warm, informal affair, and there is always a top-drawer speaker with an inspirational message.

In the crowd at every table are the vendors who share a common thread with Billy Graham—they've all been selling their products and services to his association. They've all commonly dealt with his purchasing managers and been through the grinder of competitive bidding. And now they're being told thank you as *their* customer buys them lunch. Needless to say, there are warm fuzzies in the room and the opportunity for outreach gets fulfilled.

Your annual luncheon or dinner could be celebrating the anniversary of the business, or the fifty-second anniversary of the St. Louis Browns winning the American League pennant, or whatever moves you. The important thing is that you have a group of people you want to stay in contact with, reward, recognize, or simply enjoy.

Frank owns a plating business in a large East Coast city. There are at least twelve other platers in his area. Business was a real struggle until about ten years ago, when he expanded and modernized. Now he's operating close to capacity.

His customers are mostly metal stamping places, and they come and go. Sometimes there are quality-control problems. Sometimes the customer loses his own customer for the part that Frank plates. Sometimes it's price, particularly when a new outfit rolls in and tries to buy market share by deep discounting.

One of Frank's traditions is an outdoor picnic that he's thrown for his customers and their families ever since he upgraded the business. It has always been the high point of the social season in the plating game.

Frank watches a buck pretty closely when he's at the plant, but when it comes to his annual do, he does not skimp.

He puts up tents, lays out a fancy spread, and after everyone is fully plated, the buses come and they all go to the ballgame.

The customer list includes everyone, past and present, he's ever nickel-plated for even a nickel.

Many who haven't done business with him for years are amazed he still invites them, but when they get there, Frank greets them as if they'd just placed the order of a lifetime.

"I appreciated your doing business with me in the past, and this is just a thank-you," he tells them, no matter how well, or badly, the relationship may have ended.

Frank has a rule that nobody ever talks business at these affairs, but he always makes sure he visits with each person who attends. He's told me story after story of how many former customers come back years after they've left, old scores forgotten.

Frank has been around long enough to know there's always another day, another job, and—if he stays in touch—another network of former customers.

Golf outings are among the most popular events. The thing to remember is that your network is made up of three kinds of golfers:

A. Good golfers

B. Bad golfers

C. Non-golfers

It's easy to have a format that satisfies A. However, B and C are members of your network too. I have attended many a golf event that was a blast for the good golfer but a real drag for the others. Plan the event so there is something for everyone to do—golf, tennis, swimming, poker, bridge, even just lounging in the bar, though you better make sure the bartenders are on strict orders to cut off anyone who appears to be getting fried. These events are about an afternoon of fun, not a lifetime of litigation.

Pay attention to details. Don't leave the makeup of any foursome to chance. Give the same amount of attention to seating arrangements at dinner, if there is one. If your best customer gets stuck sitting with a bore at the meal, that's too bad, but it only lasts an hour or so. If he or she gets stuck with the same jerk for eighteen holes, that's an eternity.

2. Gifts

There are three rules: Be imaginative, make it individual, make it a surprise.

Conrad Hilton, founder of the hotel chain, was a master at treating people well—and learning from his mistakes. In his book *Be My Guest,* he writes how early in his career he bagged his first big deal and, flush with the profits, bought his mother a diamond necklace.

It was expensive and far too flashy for a lady of her age and elegant taste. When he handed it to her, she burst into tears and left the room. Later she softened the blow a bit by telling her son it was a marvelous gift but far too "outstanding" for her to actually *wear.*

Hilton writes:

From that time on I began collecting and storing away little preferences that would make me a better gift giver, both personally and professionally. . . . I know that when the late and wondrous Gertrude Lawrence was a guest at our Los Angeles hotel some years later, I was tickled that I had overheard her at a theatrical party tell a friend that the tiny white roses in the corsage were her favorite flower.

And that gift [of the corsage], thoughtful rather than expensive, made such a warm impression on her that she recommended the same hotel to her friend, Noel Coward.

When I started my business career pushing broom in Charlie Ward's goldmine, the business gift of choice was calendars. Every small business got three times as many calendars as they had walls to put them on.

Most of them got pitched. The survivors seemed to be of the naked-lady variety, but you only saw those hanging next to the grease pits in the back of repair shops.

Millions of businesses still send out direct mail and promotional materials, but how many of them have any real value to the recipient?

You've got the coffee mug. You've got the T-shirt. You've got the paperweight. Or maybe you've got ten.

It takes a little imagination to cut through the clutter. How about a simple card thanking them for their friendship and patronage, accompanied by a small sample of your products? For instance, a publisher could send out a coffee-table book, a winery might send a bottle, and I know of a taxicab company that sends out a coupon book. You're an accountant? Send a brand-name pen—good for marking off tax deductions. A stockbroker? Send a "portfolio"—of the leather variety.

They'll never remember if it comes in a plain white envelope. I should know. Make it memorable.

3. Newsletters

I recently had my eyes checked. No big deal. But next thing you know, the eye doc is sending me a newsletter. It tells all about the new treatments, the latest up-to-date training, the changes that have taken place in regard to health insurance. There's even a section that pitches a program for donating eyeglasses to Third World countries.

In each issue, they spotlight a different staff member, describing the person's qualifications and training and a little bit about his or her personal life and interests. It comes complete with a nice, big, smiley picture.

What's the point of it all? Unless I start seeing spots, I'm not going to get my eyes checked any more often. I'll be happy to drop off my old reading glasses, but I've been doing that for years.

Then I realized, "Harvey, this isn't just for you, it's for the employees too. He's networking them *and* you."

I looked a little closer. Along with the maps showing office locations, emergency numbers, office hours, and the like was a monthly calendar. "May 12, Sara Carney's birthday." "May 18, Louise and Jake Austin's 30th anniversary." "May 25, Andy Farmer's 10th anniversary at the clinic." "Every Friday: Dress-Down Day." And so on.

Of course, this is the '90s version of the house organ. The purpose: to build morale among the staff, not just keep the clients informed.

How often do any of us get to see our names in the paper? It's kind of nice to be written up in a flattering way for our professional accomplishments. It's something to show to the kids and send to the folks.

It's like dress-down days. It's something to keep us loyally dropping eye drops for good old Doc forever and ever, though he never gives us a raise.

Docs aren't the only ones using newsletters. It's a device that lends itself to many businesses and professions. Some buy the newsletter from a service and have their name printed on the masthead, with space set aside for information about that particular agency. You can usually tell that Good Old Joe, the accountant, didn't write the boilerplate about 401(k)s, but so what? It's the information that you want.

The nice thing about the newsletter format is that it does double duty for a relatively modest expense.

Politicians have used newsletters for years, so they must work. Of course, unlike the ones you and I send out, they don't pay for the postage. We do.

MACKAY'S MAXIM

Don't worry that your customers aren't being properly recognized. If you're not doing it, you can bet your competition is.

Chapter 62

A FEW TRICKS OF THE TRADE— PART I

Bob Westerberg, an old friend of mine who lives in Sedona, Arizona, told me how he made customers of his small business feel appreciated. Each year, he sent a thank-you-gram to every advertiser in his publication, many of whom lived far from Arizona.

He wrote a note saying that he was sorry the airfare made it prohibitive for him to come out and take them to dinner. In lieu of being able to thank them personally, he enclosed a hand-crafted dinner chit, entitling the "bearer to two free dinners and drinks at a restaurant of his/her choice, the bill to be sent to me." There was only one hitch.

"They had to face Sedona and drink a toast to me."

Eventually Bob sold his company to a big New York outfit and stayed on for a while to brief the new people who would be running it. When he described his homespun techniques, "I was interrupted by a smirky little yuppie, who informed me, 'We don't do those things, nor do we have to.'"

Sure enough, three and a half years later, they didn't have to, because the business folded. They didn't even sell it, just folded it.

There was a happy ending for Bob, anyway. He had gotten his price and then some when he sold it.

I recently read about a local businessman, Mark Wavinak, who

opened up a Scoops Ice Cream & More. Like Bob Westerberg, he didn't have a zillion-dollar public relations budget, but he did have a little imagination.

He wrote 125 different movie stars and political figures and asked them to attend his grand opening. He told them he couldn't pay them anything, but he'd be glad to give them a free ice cream cone or ". . . we can negotiate" your fee.

Autographed photos came back from David Letterman, Frank Sinatra, Paul Newman, Clint Eastwood, Robert DeNiro, and Whoopi Goldberg, among others. Bill Clinton, who has been known to down a double dip or two, sent a letter with regrets that he couldn't make opening night but wanted to be kept "informed of any future events regarding Scoops."

New flavors? Special deals? Thirty-seven celebrities are now enshrined on the "Scoops Wall of Fame." A nice permanent addition to the decor for the cost of a few stamps, to say nothing of the extra publicity he snared when his gambit was written up in the local newspaper.

Ted Hall, a car salesman, recently moved to a dealership in the Twin Cities suburbs. He's not the first salesperson to send his customers a letter announcing his move, but he's the first one I know of to enclose a pack of flower seeds. Appropriately, they were Forget-Me-Nots.

MACKAY'S MAXIM

You don't have to have the resources of a national treasury to strike gold as a networker.

Chapter 63

A FEW TRICKS OF THE TRADE—
PART II

Not a biggie, but just one of those tricks of the trade that might come in handy.

Let's say you live in Chicago, it's the middle of August, and an important, national-scale news story is breaking in Phoenix. Now, because Phoenix is Hell on Earth in August, you wouldn't normally call. People there are irritable. All they'll do is grouse about the weather.

But here's a good and legitimate reason to renew a network acquaintance. Painlessly.

I live in a kind of reverse Phoenix: Minneapolis. August is great. I get lots of calls. No one calls me here in January.

People like me who live in strange and forbidding places make excellent network partners because we're so often ignored.

They don't call us the "flyover people" for nothing. Call us anyway. We love the attention.

> **MACKAY'S MAXIM**
> Just because the visibility is zero doesn't mean members of your network should be invisible.

Chapter 64

YOU NEVER KNOW WHEN THE PHONE IS GOING TO RING

Last month I went to my fiftieth class reunion.

(Snicker, snicker.)

I heard that!

My fiftieth *grade-school* class reunion. So I'm not quite as old as you may have thought.

Of the forty-two kids who graduated from eighth grade at Horace Mann Grade School in Saint Paul in 1946, thirty returned to their "alma mommy" for the event.

As you might expect, we're nearly all grandparents. Almost half of us still live in the Twin Cities.

We spent a wonderful evening together at a downtown club and, of course, promised to stay in touch.

It wasn't an idle promise. Amazingly, many of us have been doing it for fifty years.

I've maintained season-greeting-card-I-found-this-old-picture-in-the-attic contact with several old classmates, including one who now lives in Florida. Our only face-to-face meetings were at previous reunions. Still, the networking has paid off.

One day my phone rang and there was Gene.

"Harvey, I happen to sit on the board of the Sundance Institute out of Salt Lake City," Gene said. "They're looking for geographic balance, and the Midwest is not represented. Well, I've kind of lost

touch with my roots, except for you. Remember that picture you sent me of us playing king of the hill? We had a lot of fun together. I know you'll love this group. It's Robert Redford's brainchild, a non-profit arts organization enhancing American filmmaking. He's done a phenomenal job."

Bottom line:

Who wouldn't?

And in the ten years I've served on the Sundance Board, it's been even more fun than playing king of the hill when Gene and I were in sixth grade. It also helped me a great deal in understanding the finer points of filmmaking since my son, David, is a director.

> *I got my foot in the door at the 3M company, the largest employer in our state, the same way, courtesy of two more friends from grade school.*

Not only have I benefited from my grade-school connections, but I've been able to help others.

Five years ago a former classmate phoned me to ask for my help in finding a job for her son in San Francisco. He had just moved there, had no contacts, and wanted to work for Charles Schwab, the well-known brokerage firm. Three weeks and three phone calls later, her son started at Charles Schwab. He's still there, and he's doing so well they've asked me for more recommendations.

When you're five or ten years old, the last thing on your mind is who you may be networking with forty years later.

But it may not have been the last thing on Bill Clinton's mind.

At least two of Clinton's kindergarten pals, Webb Hubbell and Mike McCurry, became lifelong friends and wound up in his administration.

Was Clinton scrutinizing his playmates even then, checking out the sandbox, scanning the monkey bars for White House potential?

Five-year-olds take note: Before you snatch a cookie away from another kid, are you jeopardizing your future?

Do it anyway. You may regret it later, but when you're five, a cookie is a lot more satisfying than a network.

Besides, by the time you're ten, they will have forgotten all about it and you can really start to build your network.

If you haven't gone to a five-, ten-, twenty-five-, or even fifty-year reunion, give it a try. It does wonders for your memory. And it does wonders for your network too.

MACKAY'S MAXIM

You're never too old to start networking. And you're never too young either.

Chapter 65

YOU CAN'T WALK THROUGH A DOOR UNLESS YOU OPEN IT

Another way to stay focused on your networking goals is to keep a list in a notebook or in your PC of people you want to meet that you've read about or may have seen on television.

> *You'd be amazed at how many big cigars will be willing to talk with you or write to you if you simply make the effort. Hey, it's lonely at the top.*

Years ago Lori Peterson, a small-town twelve-year-old Minnesota girl, wrote a letter to her hero, Jimmy Carter, who was then president.

She wrote him and Mrs. Carter. They wrote her. She sent small gifts. They sent small gifts. She became a successful attorney. They became an ex-President and ex-First Lady. They have met several times and continue to maintain contact.

It's been going on over twenty years now.

Lori Peterson is one of the few people I know who can include a President and First Lady of the United States in their network. Not because she's a high-powered Washington pol. But because she had the guts to try.

Don't be so quick to say no for the other guy even when the other guy is the commander-in-chief. You'll be surprised how often the other guy says yes.

Chapter 66

THE WORLD'S GREATEST
NETWORKER

S o, who is the world's greatest networker?
The President of the United States.
Which president?

Any president.

Whoever is president at any given moment has made it there and succeeds or fails once in office, on the basis of his networking skills.

Presidents grub around for votes in New Hampshire snowbanks. They call their friends and their friends' friends begging for money. They bargain with members of Congress, swapping appointments and pork-barrel projects for support for their legislative programs.

They hold press conferences and try to reach beyond the hostile questioning to score points with the electorate. They travel to military installations to show their concern for the people who are risking their lives for their country. They attend funerals, go abroad, project empathy with minorities and the disadvantaged, kiss babies, visit hospitals, attend fund-raisers, listen to lobbyists and big cigars tell them how to run the country, send up trial balloons, suffer fools, point with pride and view with alarm.

In other words, they are the ultimate networkers.

The book *Truman,* by David McCullough, contains a story about Harry Truman when he was about to leave office. The Republican candidate, Dwight Eisenhower, had defeated Adlai Stevenson in the presidential election that fall. Ike had made an issue out of the failures of the Truman administration, and there was no love lost between the general and the former haberdasher.

"When Eisenhower gets here," said Truman, pointing to his desk, "he'll sit right here, and he'll say to do this, do that! And nothing will happen. Poor Ike. It won't be a bit like the army. He'll find it very frustrating."

Truman was half right.

He knew that the Constitution grants a president only a tiny fraction of what he needs to govern and that the rest depends on his ability to persuade others to carry out his wishes.

But Truman was wrong in assuming that Ike didn't have that ability. Ike succeeded as Supreme Allied Commander in World War II not because he could bark orders louder than other generals but because he could handle prickly personalities like Montgomery, Patton, Churchill, and de Gaulle.

He listened to their complaints. He mediated their disputes. He let them bask in the limelight. He flattered them. He cajoled them. He asked them for their opinions. He thanked them for their input.

And then he won the war.

And then he won the election.

This is how presidents get to be presidents.

They write thank-you notes. George Bush was known as "the Rolodex Kid." Wheelock Whitney, a friend of mine who was a classmate of Bush's, told me that Bush wrote down the name of every person he met at every precinct, city, county, state, and national political gathering he attended over a lifetime, together with "whatever" personal information. And he made a point of using that information as a creative way to stay in touch.

I know that's true because I have friends who heard Bush speak at a local political rally when he was vice president and met him briefly at a cocktail party. One of them promptly got a hand-written personal note from him that contained some factoid Bush had picked up from their meeting. The second one got a telephone call out of the blue one day when Bush was between planes at the Twin Cities airport.

Both of these people, substantial business types, have been dining out on their "close personal friendship" with "George" for the last decade and a half.

> *Bill Clinton, the first Democratic president to be reelected since FDR, told* **The New York Times** *that for most of his life, every evening before he turned in, he listed every contact he'd made that day and entered the names on 3 × 5 cards, with vital statistics, time and place of the meetings, all other pertinent information duly noted.*

Richard Nixon found a very creative way to capitalize on all the information he had collected. Say a fellow walked into Nixon headquarters and said he wanted to work for the candidate. He would be asked what he did for a living.

"I'm a barber," he might say.

"Okay, why don't you organize Barbers for Nixon? You're the president of the organization. Get a couple of your buddies and make them vice presidents. Get them to get some more people and they're presidents and vice presidents for a new chapter on the other side of town, and so on. And each of you throw fifty bucks or so into a pot. When you get a few thousand dollars together, come back, and we'll put together an ad for you to run in the state barbers' trade paper."

The umbrella organization Citizens for Nixon had a ton of these groups going. One of them, Mayors for Nixon, had hundreds of members and so much money, the Sunday before the election, they ran half-page ads in *The New York Times* and *The Washington Post*. The mayors' group included several who went on to national prominence, such as Dick Lugar, the senator from Indiana.

Politicians make the best networkers. One more story ought to hammer home the point.

Lyndon Johnson began his political career as a congressional aide in Washington. Slaving away in anonymity didn't appeal to the ambitious young Texan. He was eager to make political contacts.

Johnson was living at a cheap rooming house favored by other congressional aides. He began to take a half-dozen showers a day so he could "run into" his peers and build his network. Before long Johnson was working the rooming-house john as adroitly as some pols can work a Fourth of July picnic.

Johnson didn't waste much time after that. He soon ran for and was elected president of the congressional aides' own network, the Little Congress.

Johnson's choice of venue for networking may not have been the best place in the world to make new friends, but he had the drive to make use of even the most limited opportunity and turn it to his advantage.

Presidents push their legislative programs using networking techniques.

You may think that members of Congress can waltz into the Oval Office anytime they want, but most of them never see the president from one State of the Union speech to the next. On the rare occasions they are invited to the White House, they are like bush leaguers called up to The Show.

Many years ago, when Lyndon Johnson was president, the Republican congressional leadership consisted of Everett Dirksen of Illinois in the Senate and Charles Hallock of Indiana in the House. These two hard-bitten partisan midwestern Republicans conducted weekly press conferences, which the press dubbed "The Ev and Charlie Show." They used them to blast Johnson.

One day they had been particularly nasty about some legislation Johnson wanted. He invited the two of them to the White House for breakfast—and he got their support.

As they left to go back to the Hill, the press converged on them. "Why did you do it, Charlie?"

"He sure knows how much us Indiana boys like our bacon sliced real thick" was all the dazzled Charlie could think to say. Not only was the pork served to Hallock's liking, but the rumor is he and Dirksen left with a couple of pork-barrel projects for their districts.

This became known as the Johnson Treatment.

If you don't believe a little thing like that can determine the fate of nations, then I bet you didn't believe Newt Gingrich allowed the government to shut down because Bill Clinton made him and Bob

Dole exit from the back of Air Force One when they returned from Yitzhak Rabin's funeral.

Yes, that is how petty politics can be and how much decisions affecting billions and billions of dollars of legislation can depend on networking.

Or, as Ev used to say, "A billion dollars here. A billion dollars there. Sooner or later, it adds up to real money."

MACKAY'S MAXIM

You don't have to be in politics to be a politician. Learn from the best.

Chapter 67

AND NOW FOR THE RUNNERS-UP

Back in the 1920s, people were surprised to see a gentleman in a tuxedo emerging from a manhole on the corner of 42nd and Broadway.

The manhole man was Bruce Foraker, head of the Bell Telephone system in New York City. As he left the theater on a frigid January night, he passed a manhole where a couple of Bell employees were splicing cable, so he dropped down to have a little chat.

How do you suppose Foraker's people felt about working for him? No surprises here.

Foraker was called "the man of 10,000 friends" because his employees held him in such great respect.

A while back consultant Sarah Vander Zanden was seated next to Honeywell CEO Michael Bonsignore at a dinner. They began chatting about a state-of-the-art Honeywell thermostat just installed in her home, which she admitted neither she nor her husband had figured out how to program.

"I can help you with that," Bonsignore said. "Let me know a convenient time, and I'll come over and program it for you."

Before I included this story in this book, I called Honeywell to check on Bonsignore's title. Just dialed the number at the corporate headquarters, (612) 951-1000, and asked the operator what Mr. Bonsignore's correct corporate title was.

"Michael is CEO," she said.

"Michael? You call him 'Michael'? Honeywell has 53,000 employees."

"Excuse me. I mean Mr. Bonsignore," she replied.

"No, no, wait a minute. That's perfectly all right. I'm not correcting you. I think it's great you call him Michael."

"Well, he's a great guy," she said.

Can you imagine the kind of internal network Michael Bonsignore has with his employees? Or why he's CEO of the company?

Medtronic, Inc., is a $2.2 billion company with more than 10,000 employees worldwide. Its products are on the cutting edge of medical technology. Though the founder of the company, Earl Bakken, is in his seventies, he travels the world for the company, which now operates in 120 countries. When Medtronic opens a new office, Earl likes to sit down with the employees and explain the mission and the corporate culture.

And listen.

And answer questions.

The underlying message in all three of these cases comes through loud and clear: If we are going to succeed, we have to be able to communicate freely with each other.

We have to be able to share our concerns with each other.

We have to care about each other.

We have to be part of each other's network.

MACKAY'S MAXIM

Are you a gateway to information in your organization or a roadblock? Employees respect the former and resent the latter.

Chapter 68

JOIN THE GROUNDS CREW

Want to be a role model to your troops like Michael Bonsignore? Want to break down communication barriers between management and labor à la Bruce Foraker? Want to build a network that reaches every employee at every level of your company like Earl Bakken?

Here's the best way I know. Spend at least one week a year in the trenches—working on the line, pushing broom, toting barge, lifting bale—doing whatever are the toughest, most menial jobs the company has to offer.

It is a real morale booster for your entire crew when they see you doff your Armanis and actually do the nasty stuff they have to do to make a living for themselves and their families.

Believe me, anytime a boss will roll up his or her sleeves and actually do some grunt work, word will reach every corner of the shop.

And you know the employees will also spread the word to their network. What a great way to tell the world what you and your company stand for.

Besides, most of us who make our livings telling other folks what to do could use a little humbling experience in our lives. This is one way to get it.

MACKAY'S MAXIM

It doesn't matter how well you're leading if no one's following.

Chapter 69

PRESENT AT THE CREATION

Ah, the lonely artist. Working far into the night, probing the cosmos for inspiration, painting/composing/writing/whatever else it is creative types do. It sounds epic, mystical, and heroic. There's only one problem.

It's a myth.

Sure, nobody can do it but you, but it's not done in a vacuum. While you might not want the kiddies running around playing cowpersons and Native Americans under the table while you're writing the great American novel, that doesn't mean you don't need a network.

Great artistic efforts are often the product of "schools" or "salons."

In other words, "networks."

For example, it takes an expert to tell who painted many Old Masters, because artists and students often worked side by side to create them.

Great jazz? Musicians jamming. That's a network.

Paris in the '20s, the Algonquin Round Table, the Black Mountain College, all produced outstanding work because the writers and artists rubbed against other, figuratively and literally, exchanging ideas, criticism, and occasionally, bodies.

In the 1940s a talented group of writers emerged from the University of Minnesota *Daily*, the campus newspaper. Max Shulman was the first to score with a comic novel, *Barefoot Boy with Cheek*. Norman Katkov wrote several novels, including *A Little Sleep, A Little Slumber*. He became a successful screenwriter. Thomas Heggen's *Mr. Roberts* was a best-selling novel, a hit play, and a movie. It has often been called the best work of fiction to come out of World War II. For many years, Dorothy Lebedoff was a leading story editor in Hollywood.

I knew Shulman casually and once asked him how this tight little group all became such successful writers. "Because when I got published, they said to themselves, 'If that untalented so-and-so can do it, so can I,'" said Shulman.

Competition? Professional jealousy? In a network? Sure, why not? Creative networks often work that way. Not such a bad thing if it makes the creative juices flow.

At the advertising agency Fallon McElligott, they know creative people need the stimulation that comes from being around other creative people.

"We're in the communication business. We wouldn't be very good at it if we didn't know how to communicate with each other," said Bill Westbrooke, who is president and creative director.

What are some of the steps the agency takes to encourage networking?

1. "We always schedule meetings off the floor that the people work on. Why? So they're forced to see what's hanging on the walls outside their own area. That encourages feedback, comments, compliments, and mixing with one another."

2. "We hold quarterly meetings with the entire payroll to show *everyone* the new work that is being done, including work in progress. At these meetings, we always have one department make a full-blown presentation on what they're doing. We want everyone to have a handle on what's going on throughout the shop."

3. "Writers and art directors work in triads with designers, so they have a design perspective as well as an advertising perspective. It's very unusual in our business to do this."

4. "If you work for an advertising agency, how can you know what sells unless you've seen your agency try and sell it? Until they came to work for us, 99.9 percent of our people had never seen a full-scale presentation of an advertising pitch to a client. After we landed the McDonald's Arch Deluxe account, we gave all our people exactly the same presentation we gave to McDonald's."

5. "We gave a lot of thought to what our common areas would be like. We made a full scale replica of a diner, so that everyone would want to come and eat lunch there and goof off, take their coffee breaks, rub elbows. Too many company common areas feel like a prison mess hall."

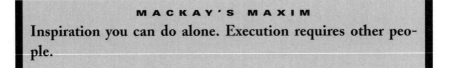

MACKAY'S MAXIM

Inspiration you can do alone. Execution requires other people.

Chapter 70

PAT O'BRIEN'S NETWORKING STORY
How to Stay in Touch

Introduction

Did you ever notice that all-seeing eye that CBS uses for its logo? I think it belongs to Pat O'Brien, who is synonymous with CBS Sports.

Pat is the networker's networker. He knows everyone. He goes everywhere. He is a human butterfly. When he lands, it's never for more than a nanosecond, because he's always on the fly to the next event. If they held a basketball tourney, a tennis tournament, and a football game, bang, bang, bang, one right after another, Pat could cover them all.

In fact, he has. After hosting this year's NCAA Final Four and the U.S. Open Tennis Championship, Pat jumped back into the studio to host CBS's coverage of college football alongside analyst Craig James.

He's also put his stamp on the 1996 Summer Olympics with a series of syndicated specials called "The Road to Olympic Gold," which he hosted with Mary Lou Retton. He guest hosts the nightly television show *Entertainment Tonight* and writes monthly columns in both *Live* magazine and *Inside Sports*. He also can be heard daily on his national radio shows, "Sportstime," "Sports Flashback," and "Sportsfan Today," as well as live on Sundays doing his national radio show "Coast to Coast with Pat O'Brien."

Easy to reach?

Hell, no!

Though we're good friends, my batting average is lower than any ballplayer who's ever appeared on one of his shows. That's okay. Pat and I know how to stay in touch, even when we have to do it by remote control.

I'm constantly forwarding messages and getting messages through Jaxie, his trusted assistant.

Phone rings. "Pat told me to call. Tell Harvey I'm thinking of him and to watch Sampras at Wimbledon if he ever wants to improve that pathetic serve of his."

Phone rings. "Harvey asked me to call. Tell Pat I just ran across an old classmate of his who went to school with him in South Dakota."

We've managed to stay in contact all these years, mostly by throwing messages over the fence, but I know he's there for me if I ever really need him.

As demonstrated by the following networking story. Thanks, Pat. I'm still working on my serve.

Pat O'Brien's Networking Story

Networking got me to the network.

It's true. I got my first job at a television network (NBC) because I knew somebody who knew Tom Brokaw. And I didn't have to be in a big city, be from a blue-chip family, or make a hundred phone calls. I simply went to the University of South Dakota and became a government major. Unknowingly, I became part of one of the greatest networking successes in higher education. His name is Dr. William O. Farber.

Doc Farber was the chairman of the Political Science Department, and his calling in life was and is networking. Each and every year, Dr. Farber takes a student under his wing. It usually is a student not living up to the potential Doc sees in him or her.

I was one of those students. So was Tom Brokaw. So was Gannett's Al Neuharth, the founder of *USA Today*. So were South Dakota Senator Tim Johnson and former South Dakota Senator Larry Pressler. So was Phil Odean, CEO of BDM, a billion-dollar corporation, plus two federal judges. So were Ken Bode of *Washington Week in Review*. So was Robert Swanson, CEO of Greyhound, Del Webb, and now with General Mills. The list is forty deep.

Through the years, the Farber network has covered public service and government, business, broadcasting, and law. His goal was to form a network so solid that no student of his ever had to go to a career-day seminar. Chosen Farber students got to borrow Doc's network of successes.

"It is surprising how you can put people together," Doc now says.

For example, in 1969, a year before I graduated, I decided I wanted to be in television. Doc reminded me that he had a student who was now the anchorman at KNBC in Los Angeles. It turned out to be Brokaw, who made one phone call and got me a job at NBC in Washington. Two days on the job and I was David Brinkley's researcher/gofer.

Farber, who is now the youngest eighty-six-year-old in America, is still sending kids out into the world. His theory is this: "No one ever reaches his or her full potential. It's not the talent you are given that counts. It's what you have done with it."

In short, any student who comes under Doc Farber's wing succeeds. I have never seen a track record like his. The network he has set up is surefire—mainly because those of us who call ourselves Farber boys (yes, there are women too) would do anything for him because he made us live up to our potential, and he helped us get to where we are today.

Three or four times a year, Brokaw, I, and company will get a call from our old professor that begins "Say, I was wondering . . ." and we respond "Whatever you need." We've sent kids to Washington, D.C.; we've set up scholarships; we've arranged meetings with his students with world figures. It is our way of paying him back, although we will always be indebted to him.

We continue to perpetuate his network, and that's all he wants. The ultimate networker doesn't want anything more than to keep the thing going. It's not a scheme. It's the way things work.

When I called Dr. Farber about this book, the first thing he said to me was "Say, I've got a student who wants to get an interview at Arizona State."

We got him the interview.

MACKAY'S MAXIM

I don't know what I'll be doing a year from now, but whatever it is undoubtedly will be based on the contacts I made today.

ALL'S WELL THAT ENDS WELL!

Chapter 71

THE TEN COMMANDMENTS OF NETWORKING

1. I will not assume that the person with the *credentials* is the person with the *power*.
2. I will not confuse visibility with credibility—mine or anyone else's.
3. I will avoid being a *schnorrer* (or a *goniff* or a *nudge,* for that matter).
4. I will never say no for the other guy.
5. I will dance with the one that brung me, bad grammar and all.
6. I will differentiate between *my* network and my *company's* network.
7. I won't stall, I'll answer the call.
8. If I don't know, or I'm not sure, I'll ask my customers and my contacts.
9. As a small business owner, I'll make "the personal touch" my mantra.
10. I'll catch the *Zeitgeist,* and when it changes, I'll catch it again.

Chapter 72

YOUR NETWORKING REPORT CARD

The biggest mistake you can ever make is to get sloppy by think-ing you're doing everything right. The only way to know how you're doing is to keep score.

How good are your networking skills?

Rate yourself. Watch the game films. Learn from your experiences. Here's a very simple test you can give yourself to find out.

Answer these questions on a 1 to 5 scale, 1 being not true and 5 being very true.

1. *I have a large network of people I can call on when I need help, advice, information, or a resource.*
1   2   3   4   5

2. *When I meet someone new, I record and file information about that person within 24 hours.*
1   2   3   4   5

3. *I add at least one new person to my network file at least once a week.*
1   2   3   4   5

4. *I follow up with new contacts immediately—writing a note, making a phone call, or sending a clipping.*
1   2   3   4   5

5. *I keep track of special things—like their family, hobbies, and achievements—that matter to my contacts.*

1   2   3   4   5

6. *I can easily find out when I was last in contact with someone by looking at my networking files.*

1   2   3   4   5

7. *When I mail something out—a résumé, sales letter, change of address—I can count on having correct name spellings, titles, addresses, for everyone in my network.*

1   2   3   4   5

8. *I know about and acknowledge special dates like birthdays, anniversaries, and holidays.*

1   2   3   4   5

9. *When I want to give a business gift, I can count on my networking file to give me an excellent idea of what the person might like.*

1   2   3   4   5

10. *I make it easy for others to add me to their networks by providing my business card, notifying them of address changes, and keeping them informed about my career progress.*

1   2   3   4   5

11. *When friends ask me for the name of a good resource on a particular subject, I am usually able to locate one from my network.*

1   2   3   4   5

12. *When the moment comes, I can usually tap into my network to wow a prospect, a boss, or potential employer with special information or an expert resource.*

1   2   3   4   5

So much for the self-survey. Here's the multiple-choice section.

13. *A particularly argumentative and hostile guy is holding forth at a business reception—one you're hosting with two of your peers. He's not wearing a name tag, so you don't know who he is or what he's doing there, and he's fixed on you as the prime member of his audience. Do you:*

   a. Interrupt the tirade and ask him his name, rank, and serial number?

   b. Wait until he stops to catch his breath and then ask for his credentials?

   c. Listen, make eye contact, and gracefully excuse yourself to greet a newcomer to the room, promising to return. Then try to find out who this guy is, hoping he's just a windbag who drifted in to get a free drink?

If you answered c), give yourself 5 big ones; 1 point for b) and zipola if a). Why get excited about a cocktail party pundit? Everyone has encountered this type before and they may be obnoxious, but they're hardly dangerous. If he's a heavyweight, you don't want to offend him, so you *will* return and hear him out, and if he isn't, the curtain will come down when the dinner bell gongs.

14. *You somehow come by a competitor's list of resources, clients, and P&Ls. Do you:*

   a. Read it and absorb as much as you can, and then ditch it in the incinerator?

   b. Photocopy it. Stash it. Read it and pass it along to your colleagues?

   c. Put it in an envelope, seal it without reading its contents, and make an appointment with its owner to return it?

   d. Put it in an envelope, seal it without reading its contents, and mail it back to its owner with an anonymous note reading "Interesting stuff. We sure will be able to use it"?

   e. Use it to discredit the person who was careless enough to leave it behind, thereby not only gaining the use of the valuable information but disrupting your competitor's operation?

Give yourself 5 if you picked c. You have created extraordinary goodwill, a clean transaction, and an additional network ally should you ever need one. You also should consider resigning your business position and answering a call to Holy Orders. Only a candidate for sainthood could have resisted taking a peek.

I'd award a 1 for choosing d. No networking value in this choice, but it proves you're personally honest, anyway, even if you have a bit of a mean streak. Picking a or b nets you a networking goose egg. If you picked e, you get −5 and a job working for Ivan Boesky.

15. *One of your best friends in the business community is having a corpo-rate-sponsored seminar, and she's the keynote speaker. Frankly, as much as you like and respect her, you know her message by heart. On top of that, there's a competing seminar with well-known keynoters whom you've never heard before and would benefit by attending. Do you:*

    a. Explain this to your friend, expecting *her* to understand?

    b. Pretend you went to her seminar and go the other?

    c. Stick with your buddy?

Five points for c. Networks are as thick as blood. There will be times and places to hear the hot shots. This is not one of them. You go to her seminar because you would want her to go to yours. *Nada* points for a, the dumb but honest answer, and −1 for b, the dumb but dishonest answer.

16. *You're in your favorite city away from home. As it turns out, you have the entire day to yourself before you have to return to work. Do you:*

    a. Go to every art gallery, museum, restaurant, theater, and sporting event you can squeeze into 24 hours?

    b. Lock yourself in the hotel room and work the phone just as if you were back at the office?

    c. Pick out a likely but as yet untapped customer, call, cold and unannounced, tell the customer you find yourself in town with some free time and he/she is the one person you want to meet, could you take him/her to lunch?

    d. Same drill as c, except it's an existing customer you haven't seen in some time, say six months?

It's d for 5. It's a lot easier to keep an old customer than it is to find a new one. Three points for c. Extra credit (2 points) if you can combine a with either c or d. Why not kill two birds with one stone and go somewhere special? Naked a gets you nothing. If you pick b you get one point—poor networking instincts, but great work habits.

Now total your score for all 16 questions and rate your network:

  0–25   Your circuits are down.
26–40   You're getting some results, but there's still too much static on the line.
41–55   Your signal is coming through, but it could be a bit stronger.
56–69   You're up and running. Keep it going.
70–82   We read you loud and clear!

MACKAY'S MAXIM
You'll never know you're winning if you don't keep score.

Chapter 73

THE PERFECT NETWORK

This network was founded in Akron, Ohio, on June 10, 1935, by a stockbroker and a doctor.

All members are equal. They come from every walk of life. To help ensure that no member feels superior or inferior to any other member, they are known to each other only by their first names and last initials.

Names, titles, standing in the community, wealth or lack of it do not matter. Only the common bond among them matters. There is no hierarchy. No chapter presidents. Leadership is an organizational task that rotates among members.

Each member is pledged to help any other member who needs help whenever that help is needed. We're talking a whole lot of 2 A.M. calls here.

Membership is voluntary. You have to want to join to become a part of this network.

Often people join, then quit, then join again.

Sometimes people are so ambivalent about becoming part of this network that they will attend scores of meeting before deciding to join.

No matter. They're still welcome.

However, this is an affinity group. There is one requirement to become a member.

You have to admit you're an alcoholic.

Alcoholics Anonymous is probably the most effective network ever devised. It's a lifelong network that takes people who are nearly six feet under and pulls them up again.

"I wouldn't be alive today if it weren't for AA," says Don B. "I know guys who have been hauled in front of a judge for drunkenness sixty times who are sober and have been sober for years because of AA."

Don B. has been a member for thirty-nine years and still attends weekly meetings.

You tell me networks are kid's stuff? Networks can produce miracles. I can show you a roomful of them any day.

Alcoholics Anonymous is the perfect "selfless" network. It doesn't offer money or advancement or fame. In fact, it promises anonymity. What it provides instead is reciprocal support in the face of the daily crisis of temptation. This is not a network that people want to join. It is one many *have* to join. Because it is selfless, AA is a great case study for harnessing the power of networks.

Shared failure and shared success function largely the same way—they strengthen those who need it the most.

MACKAY'S MAXIM

When God closes a door, somewhere God always opens a window.

Chapter 74

TEACH YOUR KIDS THE POWER OF NETWORKING

The single best reward of networking is being able to share your skills and your network with others. Especially your children.

We all do things for our kids. Or try to.

One of my offspring was looking for a part-time job while she was attending the University of Michigan. She located the job she wanted to land—hostessing at a popular campus restaurant—but a million kids had applied. She wanted me to help her hold the landing net.

I tried, believe me. But I didn't know anyone in Ann Arbor, and I just couldn't connect.

"Sorry, Jojo."

"That's okay, Dad. I've got an idea. I'm going to give it a shot. I'll let you know how it goes."

When she went in for her interview, she showed the manager a flyer she'd written. The headline read "Jojo says, 'Have I got a seat for you!' "

"If you give me the job, I'll send out this flyer to every one of my friends. Here's the list."

She held up her Rolodex and fanned the cards. There were 200 names on it.

She got the job and the restaurant got a lot of new business they would not have gotten otherwise.

MACKAY'S MAXIM

If more people knew how to network, wouldn't we all have bigger, better networks? Think about it.

Chapter 75

HAVE YOUR KIDS TEACH YOU THE POWER OF NETWORKING

After Jojo read the last item, she said, "Don't you think the headline is a tad presumptuous, Dad? I mean, the point of the story is, I did it myself. What makes you think we can't teach you stuff? Are you computerized?"

"No." (My answer in 1988, when Jojo was trying to land that hostessing job.)

I yield.

Get your kids to help you. Maybe it's computerizing your Rolodex. Maybe it's teaching you that popular music didn't end when you stopped listening to it. Or maybe it's helping you tap into their network.

People are often amazed when I tell the story about Jojo and the waitressing job.

"She had her own Rolodex? And it had 200 names?

"How did that happen?"

Because I knew my kids would eventually have to build networks. I just didn't see why they had to wait until they were adults.

Every time something interesting happened with a member of my network, I was sure to mention it at the dinner table, and it wasn't long before my three kids began to see the power of networking.

> *When my kids became teenagers, I gave them each their own Rolodex. It was one of the best things I have ever done.*

When they got their own Rolodex, I helped them capture all the information they needed about their friends and the people they met, and showed them how to stay in touch.

Soon it became a habit. And the more success they had with networking, the more deeply ingrained the habit became. So it wasn't any surprise that Jojo tapped her college network to get the job. And it wasn't any surprise she got it.

MACKAY'S MAXIM

Teaching your kids how to network is one of the best investments you'll ever make.

Chapter 76

KID POWER

Kids are like Super Glue. Don't underestimate their bonding power.

Maxine and Nancy worked in the same office and couldn't stand each other.

"She's bossy," said Maxine to her husband.

"She's careless," said Nancy to her husband.

That year they sent their sons to the same summer day camp.

Maxine's son, Trevor, was seven, a year older than Nancy's son, Grant.

Trevor doted on Grant. Trevor thought of him as the little brother he wished he had.

Grant idolized Trevor. Grant thought of him as the big brother he wished he had.

Trevor knew how to swim. Despite years of expensive swimming lessons, Grant didn't.

"Watch me, Grant," said Trevor. "I'm ducking my head in the water. If you can do this, you can learn to swim."

"I hate that," said Grant.

"I did too," said Trevor, "but it's okay once you get used to it."

"I don't know if I can," said Grant.

"Hold your breath," said Trevor.

"I'll try," said Grant.

"You're my best friend," said Trevor.

"You're my best friend too, Trevor," said Grant.

Grant held his breath and ducked his face all the way down into the water. Soon enough he learned to swim. For the rest of the camp season, Trevor and Grant went everywhere together. One day Trevor didn't feel well and didn't go out all day. Grant wouldn't go out either.

That fall Maxine came home from work one day and said to her husband, "Trevor and Grant are so cute together. Isn't it sweet how they have become such good buds? You know, Grant's mother isn't so bad after all. She seems to be lightening up a little bit."

About the same time, Nancy told her husband, "Trevor is going to sleep over Saturday night. And by the way, I think Trevor's mother is starting to do a better job with the paperwork."

It's the oldest, corniest piece of advice in the world but it still works: The strongest networks are built on friendship. Be a friend not only to the people in your network but to the people who matter the most to the people in their network.

Note and remember the names of your network's kids and spouses. Ask about them. Look for any recognition they receive and be certain to congratulate them on their achievements. A note to a business associate's newly graduated daughter, or an hour of mentoring a friend's son regarding his career choices, is worth a lifetime of friendship to their parents.

Whose picture do you carry in your wallet? Your kids or your media contact?

MACKAY'S MAXIM
And a little child shall lead them.

Chapter 77

IT ISN'T ONLY PEOPLE
WHO NETWORK

srael is a tiny country about the size of New Jersey, yet every tiny twist and turn in Israeli politics is reported in this country as if it were taking place at the local town meeting. By and large, both our media coverage and our public feelings toward Israel are favorable.

South Africa gets nearly the same kind of attention. That's another small country, halfway around the world, visited by only a handful of Americans every year, whose doings get reported meticulously in our national media. Since the dismantling of apartheid, our public attitudes toward this country also have been generally favorable.

On the other hand, the media buzzword for news from South America, our hemispheric neighbor, is "mego."

Mego is short for "my eyes glaze over." It takes a revolution to snag a line about the doings in Uruguay or Ecuador in the American media. Arab countries don't fare much better. Public attitudes tend to be skeptical and condescending.

Israel and South Africa are very open toward the media. The other countries I've mentioned are not.

Israel and South Africa, unlike others, also have very active public relations programs. They monitor U.S. politics very closely. When an opinion leader begins to emerge here, even at the lowest level of local politics or the media, you can be sure his or her ascent is noted in Jerusalem and Johannesburg.

The careers of mayors, council members, influential business people, talk show hosts, columnists, editorial writers, all are duly recorded, and usually early in their careers, these new leaders find themselves invited to an international "conference" or a "seminar"—all expenses paid—by the Israeli or South African government.

That's quite a heady trip, particularly for people who may never have been out of the United States.

They stay at first-rate hotels, meet high government officials, and see the best the country has to offer.

> *By paying attention to emerging opinion leaders before they become emerged, cynical and jaded leaders, these two semi-Third World countries have managed to put in place a hugely important network in this country that will support their policies and influence public opinion on their behalf.*

On the surface, it would seem that Israel and South Africa have very little in common. But there is a significant similarity.

For many years, they were both pariah states.

The notorious United Nations Resolution 3379 condemned Zionism—the Israeli policy of encouraging the resettlement of Jews throughout the world in Israel—as racism. South Africa was even more a political outcast, not even welcome to participate in the Olympic Games because of its discriminatory racial policies.

These two countries were dependent on their own ingenuity to make friends that were denied them because of their untouchable status in the international community.

Both of these nations became networking experts by necessity. One by one, person by person, they forged links abroad.

Among nations, networking is a big-time operation. They're playing for keeps.

MACKAY'S MAXIM

You can do what Uruguay and Ecuador still haven't figured out.

Chapter 78

Q & A

Q: *Why do you network, Harvey?*

A: Other people know other things—and other people—that I don't know.

Q: *What's a good icebreaker?*

A: There is no all-purpose line for every occasion. I know better than to try to memorize something. It sounds phony and stilted. Usually I just try to ask an interesting or fun question about the other person.

Q: *Every comic has one killer line to silence a heckler. Don't you have at least one killer networking line?*

A: Okay, there's one. When I'm with Carol Ann, and we get into a dinner conversation with a new couple at the table, I always ask: "How did the two of you meet?" Nine times out of ten you can sit back and listen for ten minutes.

Q: *What's your most recent story from that kind of encounter?*

A: I asked the question at a dinner in Atlanta when we were at the 1996 Olympic Games. The answer that came back was "I was sitting in the last row of a 747 flying from New York to Florida and Ken insisted I was in his seat. A friendly argument ensued.

We laughed and joked about it and six months later we were married."

Q: *Is networking like playing the piano and so requires concentration and discipline? Or is it like being a good party guest, in that focus and concentration aren't as good as being everywhere you can be?*

A: What you're really asking me is whether the best networkers are Mr. Inside types or Mr. Outside types, the good organizers or the good people.

Billy Graham is a great Mr. Outside. He is known and respected and admired throughout the world. We talked earlier here about "Six Degrees of Separation," how we can reach anyone anywhere through a chain of six people. Well, Billy Graham is so well known and well liked, he is probably the only person on the planet with a network that connects with anyone he wants to without any intermediary.

George Wilson was the quintessential Mr. Inside. Very few people have ever heard of him, but he's the man who, for decades, actually managed the Billy Graham organization. George's management ability, coupled with Billy Graham's vision and leadership, enabled it to grow from just Graham and Wilson to a cast of thousands.

George Wilson had proven himself as a skilled organizer through early efforts at arranging evangelistic rallies with thousands of young people. George took care of the endless details, the promotions, the mailings, the space requirements, the sound systems, while Billy was "outside," motivating millions of people through the power of his preaching.

They were able to attract a board of directors from among national corporate leaders, assemble a team of several hundred unusually dedicated and competent employees, and build a headquarters office—all of it geared to reaching a worldwide audience.

Their finances are sound, there has never been a breath of scandal attached to the operation, and while other evangelists have fallen by the wayside, the BG organization just keeps getting bigger and better in reputation and influence. Billy and George, along with their board and their team of employees, did it together—Mr. Outside and Mr. Inside.

Some networks are connected to a higher power.

Q: *Just how often are you out in the social landscape, building contacts, finding friends? Do you talk to anybody, from the guy in the airplane seat next to you to the mailman?*
A: I do, but that's me.

Q: *Does everyone you meet go into your Rolodex?*
A: No.

Q: *Then what are your criteria?*
A: Well, I have several. One is, do I go in theirs? If I do, then you can be sure they go in mine.

Beyond that, it's a combination of instinct and need. The instinct part is: Is this person interesting? Was the meeting memorable or enjoyable enough so I want to stay in touch?

Second, is this a person who knows someone or something that should be part of my network? If they meet any of those criteria, in they go.

Q: *How much time do you devote to managing or maintaining your network?*
A: Two questions for the price of one.

Okay, managing. That's full time, but full time in the sense that breathing is full time. Your antennae are always up, you're always trolling, but not in a conscious way.

Sure, there are times and occasions when you know you want to vigorously network among the people you happen to be with: You're at a convention, you're attending a civic function, you're interacting at a social event.

There are other times where things just happen. You find yourself in a conversation with a cabdriver, a waiter or waitress, the person next to you at a ballgame or on an airplane. Does it go beyond just a pleasant encounter?

It could. Depends on those three little criteria I just mentioned: Do they want to make you part of their network? Was the experience worth repeating? Do they know something or someone you don't?

Now, maintaining. If you mean paperwork, I do as little as possible. I'm a Mr. Outside. But as little as possible will take at least an hour a week dictating notes and making entries.

If you mean maintaining in terms of keeping contact, that's a constant. I'm sure I do it consciously at least an hour a day. Maybe I do it twenty-four hours a day. Should everyone? No. But I don't see how you can get away with less than an hour a week and still keep up your contacts.

Q: *Thanks, Harvey.*
A: Thank you. And you don't mind if I add you to my network too, do you? You ask good questions. Now let me ask you one. You're in the publishing business, right?

Q: *Yes. How did you know?*
A: Come on, Harriet. You're my editor on this book. You made me answer these questions before you'd publish my manuscript. I hope they help our readers. And thanks for all you've done to make this a better, more readable, more useful book.

Chapter 79

A FEW LEFTOVER NETWORKING APHORISMS I HAVE KNOWN AND LOVED
(and Begged and Borrowed and Stolen)

In my father's day, the traditional adornment of the reporter's cubicle was a girlie calendar. Since he covered the doings at the state capitol, a rather more elevated venue than the usual reporter's beat, he eschewed the slovenly look and went for a more sophisticated image. The walls of his office—or what passed for his office, a broom closet in the capitol building—were covered with "sayings."

My mother did the same thing, only she taped them on the fridge. Remember the Cracker Jack slogan, "A prize in every package." At Mackay's, it was a moral with every morsel.

I picked up the habit. Obviously.

There are worse ones.

- If I had to name the single characteristic shared by all the truly successful people I've met in my lifetime, I'd have to say it's the ability to create and nurture a network of contacts.
- You don't have to know everything as long as you know the people who do.
- As the world changes, one thing will remain constant: the relationships you develop over a lifetime.
- In my entire career I have never once heard a successful person say he regretted putting time and energy into keeping his Rolodex file.
- You can't stop the world from changing, but one thing is always within your control: the strength of your relationships with others.

- Put your memory where your mouth is. If you want to impress people with how much you care, show them how much you remember.
- The people you are closest to and need most are the ones you are most likely to take for granted.
- It's lonely at the top. The bigger they are, the more strokes they need.
- It is a myth that people do not like to be asked to help. Don't be afraid to ask.
- People don't plan to fail, they fail to plan.
- What you are is God's gift to you. What you make of yourself is your gift to God.
- Remembering doesn't work. Anyone who counts on his memory has a fool for a filing system.
- One of the greatest mistakes you can make in your career is being afraid to ask for help.
- There is no such thing as having a poor memory. You either have a trained or an untrained memory.
- Ninety percent of the people that I share my philosophies with about organizing and using the Rolodex file or software will never put them into practice. They lack the necessary ingredient: discipline.

MACKAY'S MAXIM

A good aphorism might not solve the problem, but it sure makes you feel better.

Chapter 80

SOME FINAL DOS AND DON'TS

1. Do try to recognize the differences among people in your network. Ask people who like to be in control for their opinions. Ask team players to help you solve problems.
2. Don't expect every contact you make to give you an immediate return. It takes awhile to find the gems. It may take even longer to polish them.
3. Do try to renew valuable contacts even when you've waited too long. It isn't necessary to do it all at once. Start by making a phone call just to say hello, then follow up with a face-to-face meeting.
4. Don't use your network to make a connection where there is no real connection. It's like arranging a blind date between a sixty-year-old-widow and the teenager who mows your lawn.
5. Do change your approach for each of your networks. This isn't hypocritical. You wouldn't ask your clergyman to join your Friday night poker game. And he wouldn't wear Bermuda shorts to your wedding.
6. Don't stay with one group exclusively. Expand your horizons or you'll stagnate.
7. Do learn to listen. Fran Liebowitz had the sad-but-true insight that "the opposite of talking isn't listening. It's waiting."
8. Don't hide your light under a bushel basket. If you're going to do someone a favor, let him or her know about it.

9. Do learn to distinguish between formal and informal relationships. That old football teammate may have thrown the block that freed you up for a touchdown, but you will be doing him no favor to recommend him for a situation that is inappropriate.

10. Don't presume someone is in your network when that someone isn't in your network. There are politicians who can shake your hand with both hands, look you deeply in the eyes, call you by your first name, rattle off the names of your wife and five little kiddies in order of their birth, and still honestly not remember who you are the next day. (An aide gave them all the information thirty seconds before you walked into their office.)

11. Do use other people's time constructively. Staying in touch does not mean making a pest of yourself. If you have trouble reaching members of your network by phone, then write a note. Still no response? Time to ask yourself if they're members of your network.

12. Don't let your network get stale. Find ways to stay in touch and keep people informed of your moves.

13. Do be prepared to return any favor given you. Better yet, anticipate the request by doing something unasked.

14. Don't permit anyone to use your name unless you're certain he or she won't abuse it. That's one networking favor you should be extremely wary of granting.

15. Do hoard the favors you're owed and be careful and selective about calling them in.

16. Don't burn your bridges. You're leaving to go off and conquer the world? That's great, but don't slam the door on your way out. Things happen. You could want to come back—or at least get back in touch.

17. Do keep your door open. Okay, when they left you to go off and conquer the world, they did slam the door on their way out. Not so great, but so what? Even if someone had a problem that caused me to fire her five years ago, I have been known to hire her back if she's proved she's got the problem licked. Just because someone walks out of your network doesn't mean you can't let her back in.

18. Do get a kitchen cabinet of trusted advisers. You don't want to work the high wire without a net—or a network. Unless you're one

of the Flying Wallendas, you need a trusted crew who can help you get back on your feet if your giant leap falls short.

19. Don't abandon someone who's out of the loop. Next year that person may be directing the loop. Up-and-down cycles are part of life. I've known many real estate developers who have gone broke at least once. Richard Nixon rose from the dead more times than Elvis.

20. Do be a *mensch*. The best way you can help yourself is to use your network to help others.

DRINKING FROM THE WELL . . . AND SHARING THE WEALTH!

Chapter 81

STANLEY MARCUS' NETWORKING STORY
What Goes Around Comes Around

Introduction

Stanley Marcus has more sheer energy, enthusiasm, and curiosity than anyone I know. Fortunately, he is just reaching his prime. He's only ninety-one.

This remarkable man is known worldwide. His name appears on every Neiman Marcus store, where he served for many years in various executive positions, including chairman of the board, CEO, and president.

He is a Renaissance man who has written several books, including *Minding the Store,* and countless articles. He is an active consultant on retailing to major corporations, is in demand as a keynote speaker to business and cultural groups, knocks out a weekly newspaper column, is an expert and active collector of Native American and Spanish Colonial art, and works out three days a week with a trainer on a stationary bike.

If all that doesn't tire you out, I don't know what will. In short, he's ninety-one years young and still going strong.

Stanley Marcus' Networking Story

Each of us, I am sure, has a personal opinion about networking. I happen to believe that the process is one that comes spontaneously out of a genuine desire to be helpful to another individual to solve a problem.

I don't believe in doing something to invite reciprocation, for I get a great personal gratification by being useful and helpful. Still, I've come to believe that good deeds do indeed come back to you—even though it may take many years. Here are a couple of incidents that are illustrative.

Shortly after World War II, my wife and I were asked to entertain a group of Asian teenagers who were being brought to this country to acquaint them with American lifestyles. They were from all parts of the Asian continent—Thailand, Cambodia, India, Pakistan, Burma, Laos, and Vietnam.

It was a fascinating group of kids that we entertained at our home along with our own teenage children and some of their friends. A young student from India was interested in advice about how to get into an American university with strong programs in international trade. I was able to arrange for interviews for him with several such schools, and eventually he ended up at Columbia University.

I kept up with him over his college career by sending him books and magazines on India and its problems. Time passed on, and I lost track of him.

In 1964 I made my first trip to India, trying to organize a cooperative trade promotion venture for Neiman Marcus that would promote Indian products and culture. When I went to New Delhi, I found myself lost in a sea of bureaucracy. Everybody liked the idea, but no one would commit himself or the government to do anything but think about the proposition.

Finally I was taken in to see the vice-minister of trade. After introducing myself to him, he beamed with a warm smile and an out-stretched hand and reminded me that he was my young Indian student friend. I hadn't recognized him.

He immediately took charge and led me through the labyrinthine channels of the Indian government's policy structure. In four days we forged an agreement that enabled the project to get off the ground.

If I hadn't met up with him, I might have stayed in India for four years without results.

Second example:

Prior to World War II, "Jock" Lawrence, a young executive for Metro-Goldwyn-Mayer, came to Dallas to promote a new motion picture. He was having difficulty getting a booking at the most important movie house because of some previous disagreement. I offered to introduce him to the chief booker and smoothed the way for a reconciliation. He was deeply appreciative.

I didn't see Jock again until my first postwar trip to Paris in 1946. I ran into him at the Ritz Bar by sheer accident. By then he was Colonel Jock Lawrence, on General Eisenhower's staff.

He asked if I had ever met Ike, and I told him no. He said I must meet him, and he would arrange it. I demurred, not wanting to waste the general's time, but Jock was adamant and set the whole thing in motion.

On my arrival at headquarters, Jock was not there, but another officer ushered me into the general's office and introduced me as Stanley Marcus of Neiman Marcus.

Ike obviously had not been briefed. He looked at me, smiled, and quizzically repeated "Neiman Marcus" several times, as if he were trying to determine whether it signified a law firm or a team of acrobats. When I realized his quandary, I explained that Neiman Marcus was one of the finest specialty stores in the country and that I was on a mission to reestablish our buying connection in Europe.

"You'll have to pardon me," he said, "I've been away from the U.S. so long, and even when I was there, I never had occasion to visit stores. I always shopped at the base PX."

He asked me to explain in more detail about our operation, after which I said, "General, I hope you will decide to seek the nomination for the presidency, and if you succeed, I hope you will be elected."

He thanked me but was noncommittal about his intentions.

As I left, I said, "General, if you do decide to go for the nomination and get it, and if you are elected, I hope that as an ex-Texan, you will buy Mrs. Eisenhower's inaugural gown from us."

He laughed and replied, "If I do, I will."

He was true to his word, and when he was elected president, we furnished the inaugural gown, made by one of our leading dressmakers, Nettie Rosenstein.

Being nice to people is good networking—besides, it gratifies the soul.

Chapter 82

CALL JACK

I wrote a story early in this book about my father, Jack Mackay, and his network. I'm going to end the same way.

Here is an excerpt from Rabbi Max Shapiro's eulogy for my father: "Call Jack."

All of us have a story. Each of our lives would make a book, for our emotions, our drives, our achievements are all unique and singular. Bits and pieces of Jack's story can be found in his writings about the Dillinger gang, the Hamm kidnapping, the great and bloody Minneapolis truck strike, his long nineteen-year effort to free Leonard Hankins, an innocent man who had been convicted of murder.

Jack had the great ability to make friends—friends in every walk of life. I talked to many of them, and when I asked them about Jack, I received the same answer, "When we needed something, when there was nobody else we could go to for help, when there were problems, we would call Jack."

A victim of the concentration camp is seeking his family and red tape abounds. Call Jack—and the red tape vanishes.

A man must be admitted to a hospital and beds are not available for six months. Call Jack—and a bed is somehow found.

Money is needed to guarantee funds for a refugee from Hitler. Call Jack—and funds are available.

A child needs a special school, but conditions make it impossible to accept her. Call Jack—and acceptance comes through.

A man needs a job, and no jobs are available. Call Jack—and the man goes to work.

Jack was a man with many concerns. And each concern meant human beings. How many said "Call Jack"—call Jack for this, call Jack for that—we will never know. How many he helped we will never know.

And perhaps—just perhaps—God had a task, a task difficult to do, a task that needs resourcefulness and tenacity—that needed careful planning. And God too must have pondered and reluctantly must have said "Call Jack."

I hope your network can help you find a job or earn a promotion or close a sale or make a buck. But even if it never does, if your network can do what Jack Mackay's did—if it can help you help someone who needs it—then you have the best network of all.

Chapter 83

THE LAST WORD

Finished with the book?

Give it to someone in your network. Or swap it with him. (Just don't tell my publisher.)

INDEX

If you have thoughts, comments, or ideas about this book, I'd love to hear from you. (Please, no requests for personal advice.) Write to me at the following address:

Mackay Envelope Corporation
2100 Elm Street Southeast
Minneapolis, MN 55414

I also can be reached electronically. My E-mail address is Harvey@Mackay.com. My Web Site address is http://www.mackay.com.